LIFE NATURE LIBRARY

THE
BIRDS

TIME
LIFE
BOOKS
®

LIFE WORLD LIBRARY

LIFE NATURE LIBRARY

TIME READING PROGRAM

THE LIFE HISTORY OF THE UNITED STATES

LIFE SCIENCE LIBRARY

GREAT AGES OF MAN

TIME-LIFE LIBRARY OF ART

TIME-LIFE LIBRARY OF AMERICA

FOODS OF THE WORLD

THIS FABULOUS CENTURY

LIFE LIBRARY OF PHOTOGRAPHY

LIFE NATURE LIBRARY

THE
BIRDS

by Roger Tory Peterson
and the Editors of
TIME-LIFE BOOKS

TIME-LIFE BOOKS   NEW YORK

About the Author

Roger Tory Peterson's first ambition was to be a painter of birds, but feeling that he could not make a living at that, he went to art school in the hope of succeeding as a commercial artist. Birds, however, remained his passion. He took a job with the National Audubon Society, painted birds when he could, and eventually was able to persuade a publisher to put out a bird guide full of his own illustrations and introducing a new system of field identification. This is now known wherever birds are studied as the Peterson System. It has revolutionized bird watching and made its inventor the best-known ornithologist in the world. The first Peterson *Field Guide*, which was devoted to birds of America, was followed by others on a dozen different countries. All together, they have sold nearly two million copies.

This extraordinary success has enabled the man who "couldn't make a living painting birds" to travel all over the globe, observing, painting and photographing his favorite creatures. Along the way he has written and lectured widely and is a past or present officer of 18 leading ornithological organizations. He has been awarded the Brewster Medal of the American Ornithologists Union, the John Burroughs Medal, the Geoffrey St. Hilaire Gold Medal (France) and the Gold Medal of the New York Zoological Society. He holds honorary degrees in science from Franklin and Marshall College and Ohio State University. Married, he lives in Old Lyme, Connecticut.

ON THE COVER: A white tern flutters to a landing on Midway Island. Unlike other terns it balances its egg on the bare branch of a tree, not bothering to build a nest.

Contents

TIME-LIFE BOOKS

EDITOR
Jerry Korn
EXECUTIVE EDITOR
A. B. C. Whipple
PLANNING
Oliver E. Allen
TEXT DIRECTOR   ART DIRECTOR
Martin Mann   Sheldon Cotler
CHIEF OF RESEARCH
Beatrice T. Dobie
PICTURE EDITOR
Robert G. Mason
Assistant Text Directors:
Ogden Tanner, Diana Hirsh
Assistant Art Director: Arnold C. Holeywell
Assistant Chief of Research: Martha T. Goolrick
Assistant Picture Editor: Melvin L. Scott

PUBLISHER
Joan D. Manley
General Manager: John D. McSweeney
Business Manager: John Steven Maxwell
Sales Director: Carl G. Jaeger
Promotion Director: Beatrice K. Tolleris
Public Relations Director: Nicholas Benton

LIFE NATURE LIBRARY

EDITOR: Maitland A. Edey
Associate Editor: Percy Knauth
Assistant to the Editor: Robert Morton
Designer: Paul Jensen
Staff Writers: Dale Brown, Barbara Elias,
Peter Meyerson
Chief Researcher: Martha T. Goolrick
Researchers: Gerald A. Bair, Doris Bry, Peggy Bushong,
Eleanor Feltser, Susan Freudenheim, Mary Louise
Grossman, LeClair G. Lambert, Paula Norworth,
Paul W. Schwartz, Phyllis M. Williamson

EDITORIAL PRODUCTION
Production Editor: Douglas B. Graham
Quality Director: Robert L. Young
Assistant: James J. Cox
Copy Staff: Rosalind Stubenberg, Joan Chambers, Florence Keith
Picture Department: Dolores A. Littles, Sue Bond
Assistants: Mark A. Binn, Eric Gluckman

The text for this book was written by Roger Tory Peterson, the picture essays by the staff. The following individuals and departments of Time Inc. helped produce the book: LIFE staff photographers Alfred Eisenstaedt, Eliot Elisofon, Fritz Goro, Dmitri Kessel, Leonard McCombe and Francis Miller; Editorial Production, Robert W. Boyd Jr., Margaret T. Fischer; Editorial Reference, Peter Draz; Picture Collection, Doris O'Neil; Photographic Laboratory, George Karas; TIME-LIFE News Service, Murray J. Gart; Reprints staff: Paula Arno (editor).

Introduction

SINCE birds, like men, are largely diurnal creatures and share with us the familiar daytime world of color and sound, our association with them is, not surprisingly, a long and intimate one. Man has always had a double interest in birds—on the one hand esthetic, personal, impractical; on the other, utilitarian. The latter has changed with the times and with the sum of human knowledge. Long ago, when superstitions and priestly cults were the "science" of the day, the flights of birds were carefully studied for omens, as were their entrails. For centuries man tried to probe the mysteries of flight. Although he never succeeded in duplicating the effortless, endlessly flexible aerial mastery possessed by birds, he does share the air with them today. That leads inevitably to the problems of navigation and space travel, and we find ourselves turning to the birds again—for evidence is accumulating that they chart their courses, during migration, by the sun and stars. Will we learn anything about navigation from them? Conceivably, although it is likely that we will succeed only in developing something which, in comparison to the way the birds do it, will turn out to be as crude and expensive and inflexible as a propeller-driven plane when compared to a feathered wing.

Birds have helped men for thousands of years, from the geese whose warning cries saved Rome to the canaries that were used to warn coal miners of methane gas leakage. From research currently under way, there is some reason to believe that birds may continue to provide this kind of lifesaving service by warning us that the doses of chemicals and radioactive particles that we eat, drink, breathe and absorb day after day may be reaching dangerous levels. Truly, birds touch us in unexpected places. They are far more to us than ducks and pheasants to be shot, or chickadees and cardinals to brighten a suburban winter.

As a gifted painter of birds, and in a sense creator of the modern system of field identification of birds, Roger Peterson should not be expected to master other skills. And yet he is an accomplished photographer. I once spent a day with Roger in Rhodesia as he photographed greater kudus, lilac-breasted rollers, African lions and other assorted fauna. I was struck by his care and persistence, and I suggest to the reader that he turn to the picture credits on page 186 of this book to find examples of Roger's skill with the camera. Here is a man who can do everything, including write. Small wonder that the editors of TIME-LIFE BOOKS were delighted to have him as the author of this fine volume.

DEAN AMADON
Lamont Curator of Birds, Chairman of the Department
of Ornithology, The American Museum of Natural History

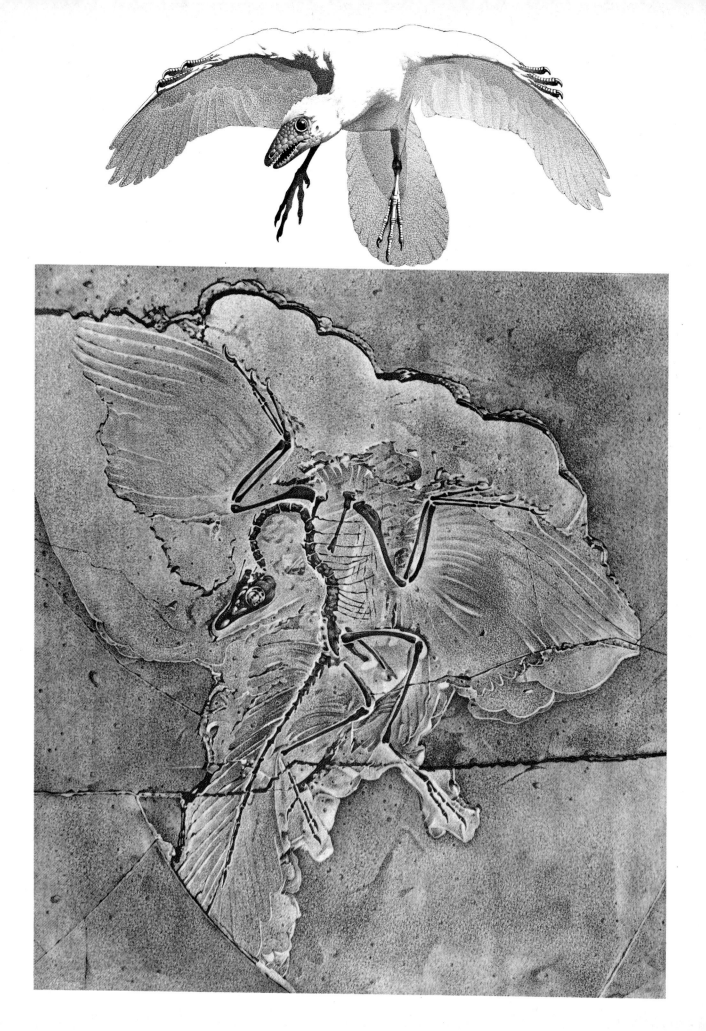

1

From Archaeopteryx to Sparrow

WHAT manner of creatures are birds? Certainly, of all the higher forms of life, the vertebrates, or backboned animals, they are the most beautiful, most melodious, most admired, most studied—and most defended. They far outnumber all other vertebrates except fishes and can be found virtually everywhere throughout the world, from the edges of the polar icecaps and the highest Himalayan and Andean slopes to the roughest seas, the darkest jungles, the most barren deserts and the most crowded cities. The center of the Antarctic continent is the only place on the world's surface where birds have not been found. Some even invade the fishes' environment to a depth of 100 feet or more, while others hide in caves so dark that they must employ a sort of built-in sonar to find their way about.

Nearly a century ago T. H. Huxley called birds "glorified reptiles." This term may grate harshly on the ears of gentle souls who keep parakeets or feed cardinals at the window, but there is much to support Huxley's contention. Birds share many characteristics with reptiles—certain skeletal and muscular features, similar eggs, an "egg tooth" on the upper jaw at hatching time, to name just a few. But the unique feature that sets them apart from all other

FOUR FOSSIL BIRDS

ICHTHYORNIS

After 50 million years birds had come a long way from the reptilian Archaeopteryx. Ichthyornis was about the size of a pigeon and probably looked somewhat like a modern tern. It lived on the shores of North America's great inland sea about 100 million years ago and was probably a skillful flier, but had small weak legs.

HESPERORNIS

Hesperornis also lived 100 million years ago on America's inland sea. It resembled a modern loon, with legs set well to the rear. A strong swimmer, it had only rudimentary wings and could not fly. Its beak was lined with sharp reptilian teeth. More than one Hesperornis species evolved, the largest being the size of a small seal.

animals is that they have feathers. All birds have feathers, and no other creatures possess them.

Considering the fact that life on earth extends back into the spectrum of time for more than two billion years, birds are a latter-day creation. Paleontologists believe that they began to branch off from reptilian stock sometime about 150 million years ago, shortly after the first mammals.

The oldest known bird in the fossil record dates back to the late Jurassic period, about 140 million years ago, and although there must have been still earlier birds or subbirds, this one has a dramatic significance all its own. It was brought to light in a slate quarry at Langenaltheim, Bavaria, in 1861, and would have been classified as a reptile except for the unmistakable imprint of feathers. The discovery was a scientific bombshell. Only two years before, in 1859, Charles Darwin had published his then controversial work, the *Origin of Species*—and here was beautifully imprinted proof of his new theory, a missing link from the past: evidence that birds had evolved from reptiles. The fossil was named *Archaeopteryx*, meaning "ancient wing." In 1877 a second skeleton was discovered about 10 miles away and in 1956 a third was found.

Although not quite a bird in the modern mold, *Archaeopteryx* was certainly not a true reptile. Its head, however, was lizardlike, with toothed jaws, its slender tail with many movable vertebrae was skeletally like that of a reptile, and its wing bones terminated in three slender, unfused, clawed fingers. Still, it had *feathers*.

Archaeopteryx probably did not fly easily. If we rationalize from its appearance, we might assume that it ran over the ground on strong legs and clambered up rocks, shrubs and trees with the assistance of its clawed wing-fingers. Its rounded wings and long but rather wide tail suggest that it was a glider that launched itself only for short distances, like a flying squirrel. It is perfectly clear, from studying its anatomy, that it could not have flown very well. We can easily imagine the predicament which led to the fossilization of the three individuals so long ago. They were probably forced into reluctant flight by some pursuing reptilian predator, only to flop down on the water and mud from which they could not rise.

To this day, *Archaeopteryx lithographica*, which was about the size of a pheasant, remains the only known species representing the subclass archaeornithes, or "ancestral birds," and we can only guess at the type of reptile from which it descended. This may have been one of the thecodonts, the possessor of long hind limbs on which it ran semierect, using its long tail as a balance.

Concurrently, also during the Jurassic, another reptilian experiment in flight resulted in the pterodactyls, which flew on slender batlike wings of skin. Though these creatures developed certain birdlike features such as beaks and light, pneumatic bones, they were not destined to survive. The Cretaceous period, which started about 135 million years ago and ended roughly 63 million years ago, saw their proliferation and also their demise while witnessing the rise of the "true birds."

These were the neornithes, birds such as *Hesperornis*, a toothed diver resembling a huge flightless loon four or five feet long, and *Ichthyornis*, a small ternlike sea bird. Their remains were discovered in the Cretaceous shales of Kansas. A cormorantlike bird also lived during this period and a primitive flamingo has been found in Scandinavia, so it is obvious that water birds had already diverged widely in form and adaptation by this time.

The current era is often called the Age of Mammals, as distinct from the Age of Reptiles, which drew to a close with the exit of the dinosaurs and pterosaurs. The early part of this era, the Paleocene and Eocene, 63 to 36 million years ago, was a time of great development which saw the ascendancy of birds over reptiles. Many of the modern orders of birds emerged—including an ancestral ostrich, and primitive pelicans, herons, ducks, birds of prey, fowl-like birds, shore birds, owls, cranes and others. As we advance further, through the Oligocene and Miocene, 36 to 13 million years ago, we find many modern genera appearing, birds very similar to present-day forms. A modern bird watcher, stepping back into time about 20 million years to scan a Miocene lake with his binoculars, would spot many familiar-looking individuals but none that he could match precisely with those of today. But there also existed certain other birds that were in blind alleys; for example the phororhacids, huge flightless birds with massive heads nearly as large as those of horses. These fearsome fowl left no modern descendants.

During the Pliocene, 13 to 2 million years ago, many species emerged that fly on earth today—species that can claim antiquity far greater than that of man. This was the period when birds enjoyed their greatest variety. Pierce Brodkorb of the University of Florida estimates that about 11,600 species were living contemporaneously, a third more than exist today.

The Pleistocene, lasting one or two million years, when man was slowly coming into his own, was a time of pressure and extermination. The world was playing hot and cold with living things, alternating between glaciation and benign interglacial periods. The great ice sheets eliminated many plants and the birds scattered accordingly.

Today the number of species of birds on earth is usually estimated to be about 8,580, give or take a few score and depending on which systematist you choose to accept. The total number of extinct species described from fossil evidence is in the neighborhood of 800—less than 10 per cent of the living species.

DIATRYMA

A 60-million-year-old flightless giant of the North American plains, this bird stood seven feet tall and had a head as large as that of a horse. Its huge sharp bill and powerful legs suggest that it was a predator that lived by running down small reptiles and mammals, in much the same way as the secretary bird does today.

ACTUALLY, any paleontologist will point out that this does not give even a remotely true picture of the number of species that have existed during the last 140 million years. Birds, with their fragile, hollow bones do not lend themselves as well to fossilization as mollusks with hard shells or mammals and large reptiles with their relatively solid bones. The road from *Archaeopteryx* to modern birds is paved with genesis and extinction. Species have arisen, have had their day and have faded away or given rise to new forms better adapted to a changing world. Recently Brodkorb, drawing on his knowledge of fossil history, came up with a tentative, over-all figure of 1,634,000 species, past and present. The living birds made up scarcely more than one half of one per cent of this total. The others have followed *Archaeopteryx* into the void.

The biologist often speaks of "adaptive radiation." This means, in the evolutionary sense, that the descendants of a single species of animal may adapt to a number of new environments or modes of life. By so doing, they "radiate," changing in form and structure away from the ancestral type to a number of divergent types.

Adaptive radiation was strikingly revealed to Darwin when his research vessel, the *Beagle*, dropped anchor at the Galápagos Islands 600 miles off the coast of Ecuador in 1835. Here he found a complex group of small, dark, finchlike birds now known as the Geospizinae. They were similar enough to be recognizable as a group that had presumably descended from a single source, perhaps some

PHORORHACOS

Related to Diatryma and with a similar predatory bill and rudimentary wings, Phororhacos was somewhat smaller—about as tall as a man. It lived in South America 30 million years ago, unhindered by the large predatory mammals that later emerged there. The modern cranelike cariama of South America may be akin to it.

EARTHBOUND REPTILE TO AIR-BORNE BIRD

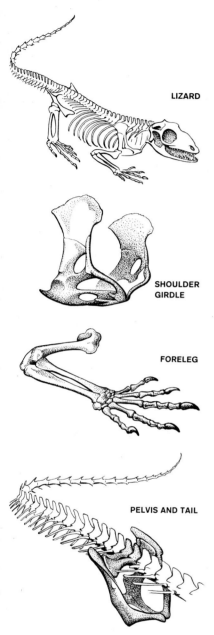

LIZARD

SHOULDER GIRDLE

FORELEG

PELVIS AND TAIL

Although descended from the same reptilian ancestors, lizards and birds have diverged considerably in structure. A typical lizard today has a long backbone and an even longer tail. Its solid frame and stout limbs, with many movable bones, are well suited to its four-footed gait.

Its shoulder girdle is strong, made of three heavy bones, but the breastbone is shallow, since large chest muscles are not needed by lizards. Short sprawling forelegs give the lizard a built-in crouch, but it uses an ankle of many elements and a five-toed foot to run swiftly. The pivot point of body weight is the pelvis. Up to 100 tail vertebrae provide rear balance.

seed-eating ground finch carried by the wind to these remote islands. Perhaps a small flock made the sea passage together. Surviving, these first wind-borne immigrants found no other small birds to offer competition. Environmental niches were empty, so eventually the colonists, prospering and increasing, adapted to various modes of existence. When Darwin made his historic visit he found that some Geospizinines were seedeaters as their ancestors are presumed to have been, but that others fed on insects, still others on cactus and one form even filled the role of a woodpecker. Their bills varied from thin, warblerlike bills to very thick beaks like those of grosbeaks. They had, in fact, evolved so as to exploit virtually every feeding opportunity the islands offered to small birds.

When we discuss Galápagos finches we are talking about relatively recent radiation. Consider the extraordinary radiation from *Archaeopteryx* to the bewildering array of modern birds.

EVOLUTION is a fluid process which can be represented by a two-dimensional family tree, but more accurately it is three-dimensional, with many twigs and branches dying off while others, reaching out in all directions, continue to modify and grow. The 8,580 species of birds on earth today represent growing twig ends. They are separate entities, populations that for one reason or another normally do not or cannot interbreed with each other. They are reproductively isolated. This large galaxy of living species has been arranged by systematists into 27 living orders of birds and these in turn have been broken down into some 155 families.

No one ornithologist has ever seen all the world's species in life—or even all of the families, except possibly in zoos. In fact, few are familiar in life with every order. For it is indeed an amazing diversity that exists in the world's population of birds, from the fragile hummingbird weighing less than a penny to the ponderous ostrich weighing more than 300 pounds.

Several of the lower orders of birds cannot fly—the ostriches, the rheas, the cassowaries and emus, the kiwis and the penguins. This gave rise to a theory that modern birds did not all come from a common ancestor, but represented two lines of descent—one that had long ago attained flight and one that is not yet off the ground. Those who held this view theorized that the ostriches and other ratites (flightless, running birds with no keel on the breastbone), as well as the penguins, never had been able to fly and were still evolving their wings. However, this view has now been written off and it is accepted that these flightless birds did have flying ancestors but lost the use of their wings because flight was no longer useful to their mode of life. In fact, flight becomes impossible for creatures as ponderous as the ratites, birds large and heavy enough to fill the niche of grazing animals.

Although the ostrich, with its heavily muscled bare thighs, is the largest living bird, even larger species were seen by primitive man not many centuries ago. These were the moas (*Dinornis*) of New Zealand and the elephant birds (*Aepyornis*) of Madagascar. The largest of the moas, like a huge pinheaded ostrich, stood 12 feet tall and is estimated to have weighed 520 pounds. Moa "graveyards" containing hundreds of skeletons have been found in New Zealand and certain of the smaller moas were still numerous a thousand years ago when New Zealand's first settlers arrived. There is evidence that one species existed in the South Island into the 18th Century.

Less is known about the elephant birds, which some like to speculate were Marco Polo's rocs. They were even more heavily built than moas and may have weighed as much as half a ton. Whether man destroyed the last of the elephant birds and, if so, how recently, is not known. Early travelers to Madagascar described *Aepyornis* eggs which were used as flasks by natives. A few such flasks are still in existence and they hold two gallons of liquid.

The ostrich, the giant among living birds, attains a stature of eight feet. It lives the life of a grazing animal, roaming in little parties over the African veldt in the company of zebras, wildebeests and gazelles. It has the distinction of being the only bird with two toes, one much reduced in size, suggesting that this fleet-footed monster, which can run as fast as 35 miles per hour, is on its way to acquiring a one-toed foot like the horse.

The two rheas, often called the "South American ostriches," are superficially like their African counterpart, but they have three toes and feathered thighs, and lack the ostrich's handsome plumes. Nevertheless, as they race across the pampas, they give much the same effect as small ostriches.

Australia also has its ratites, or ostrichlike birds—the emus and the cassowaries. They, too, are without the ostrich's plumage, and they have even more rudimentary wings and a hairy, almost shaggy look. Australian farmers hold a perpetual grudge against the fast, 120-pound emu because it damages fences and raids crops. Less often seen are the related, forest-dwelling black cassowaries of northern Australia and New Guinea. Papuan natives have a cautious respect for these temperamental birds which have been known to disembowel men with quick slashes from the long, daggerlike nails on their inner toes.

The strangest and perhaps most primitive of all the ratites are the kiwis of New Zealand. Certainly they are the most unbirdlike of all birds, shmoolike creatures shaped like large, hairy footballs and practically devoid of external wings. They have whiskery faces and nostrils placed at the very tips of their long beaks, the better to locate worms during their nocturnal forays. The kiwi's enormous five-inch egg weighs nearly a pound, one fourth to one third of the bird's body weight. Contrast this with the six- to eight-inch ostrich egg, which weighs only one sixtieth as much as the female!

FROM Mexico southward throughout most of the South American continent live the tinamous—chunky, almost tailless birds that lay deeply colored eggs so glossy that they look like porcelain. These ground birds with the haunting, whistled cries look strikingly like partridges, but are not even distantly related to them. Evolution often results in unrelated birds looking rather similar, especially when they fit a similar environment—a phenomenon called "convergence," the opposite of radiation. Tinamous are low in the family tree of living birds, supposedly close to the flightless ratites, but they still have the ability to fly.

The torpedo-shaped loons and the smaller, lobe-footed grebes are both foot-propelled divers with feet placed far back toward the tail. At first glance they would seem to belong to the same order. Actually, they are quite unrelated, coming from different ancestral lines—another example of convergence.

Penguins cannot fly, yet they have a strongly keeled breastbone and powerful flight muscles. Here, the wings have evolved into flippers, and penguins literally fly through the water, using their fleshy feet as rudders. Because their upright posture, waddling gait, dangling flippers and frock coats all add up to a lovable caricature of *Homo sapiens*, penguins have always appealed to humans. All but one of the 15 living species are birds of the cold seas of the Southern Hemisphere.

Oddly enough, the flightless penguins may have evolved from the same

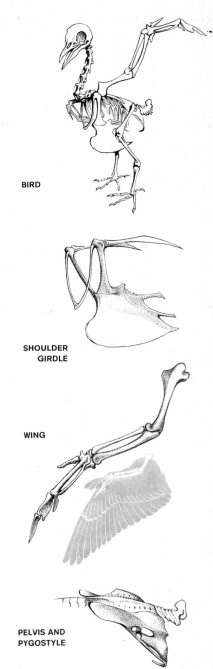

BIRD

SHOULDER GIRDLE

WING

PELVIS AND PYGOSTYLE

Compared to a lizard, a bird is a light-weight flying machine of few skeletal parts. Body bones flattened and welded onto a short backbone support the wings.

The collarbones are fused into a single "wishbone." The breastbone has a deep keel to provide a surface for attachment of large flying muscles. The wing is a lengthened forelimb. As shown in color, the arm carries the short flight feathers. The wrist and three-fingered hand together support the long primaries. The pelvic bones and lower backbone form a rigid unit. The tail feathers are anchored in the fleshy "pope's nose," close to the pygo-style, a fused remnant of the lizard's tail.

ancestral stock as the albatrosses, the supreme masters of flight. Students point out that they have in common a beak made up of horny plates, quite unlike the simple sheathlike bills of most other birds. Eons of evolution have made one an avian submarine, the other a sailplane.

Albatrosses, petrels and shearwaters all belong to the order of "tube-nosed swimmers," so called because the nostrils, unlike those of most other birds, are in short tubes on the sides or on the top of the bill. They are the blue-water seaman's companions and range in size from the swallow-sized black-and-white storm petrels to the wandering albatross, whose wings span more than 11 feet. Although they roam all oceans, the majority of species live in the Southern Hemisphere and are especially numerous between the Antarctic ice pack and the southern tips of the continents.

The word albatross was an English corruption of *alcatraz*, the name the Portuguese seaman applied to all large sea birds, especially pelicans. Pelicans, however, are not closely related to albatrosses; they belong to the next great order of birds, the "totipalmate swimmers," which differ from all other web-footed birds by having the hind toe joined to the front three by a web. They also have throat pouches, relatively small in the boobies, cormorants, anhingas and frigate birds, but enormous in the pelicans—some of them have a pouch capacity of nearly three gallons. All birds of this order are fisheaters; most but not all are marine.

Modern birds, adapting and changing during the last 100 million years, have filled virtually every available niche in the world. About 120 living species of "long-legged waders" have evolved. These birds—the herons, storks, ibises and related birds with stiltlike legs for stalking the shallows and long compensating necks—make their living catching small fish, frogs and other forms of aquatic life. Bills take a variety of shapes—daggerlike or spearlike, upturned, downturned, shoelike and even spoonlike.

The most specialized of all the wading birds are the colorful flamingos. Students hotly debate whether they are more closely related to storks, which they superficially resemble, or to geese. Their gooselike cries, gooselike young, their molts and even their feather parasites suggest an affinity with geese. Certainly they have developed a way of life unique among birds, evolving grotesquely exaggerated necks and legs and thick, bent bills equipped with fringed lips for straining edible organisms from the souplike mud in which they wade.

The waterfowl, the familiar web-footed swimmers which form the sportsman's game, include the ducks, geese and swans. The distinctive feature that most of the 146 species have in common is a flattish "duck" bill, although the mergansers, or fish ducks, are equipped with sawlike mandibles. Some ducks dabble, others dive for a living, while swans, with necks longer than their bodies, dip or tip up for their diet of aquatic plants. Geese, shorter-necked, also do this but primarily graze on land for grass and roots.

Among the most spectacular of all groups are the birds of prey. Superbly designed for their predatory task, they are powerful fliers, capable of effortless soaring or plunging bursts of speed. There are over 270 living species in this order. All have hooked beaks for tearing flesh, and those which take living prey characteristically have strongly hooked talons. Vultures, those naked-headed birds of prey which feed on carrion, have weaker feet—an obvious adaptation, since their prey cannot escape. Owls, though nocturnal birds of prey, are not included in this order; more will be said about them later.

The fowl-like birds, numbering about 250 living species, embrace the grouse, turkeys, quails, partridges, pheasants, currassows, guans, mound builders and the primitive hoatzin. They are sturdy ground birds, with grubbing bills and stout, scratching toes. Some are among the world's most gorgeous birds; others, notably the domestic fowl, are among the most economically important.

The cranes, rails, coots, bustards and related families, some 185 species in all, belong to an order that, for convenience, we might call "marsh birds." The stately cranes are storklike, whereas rails and coots are more like hens and hide in the reeds. The bustards are heavy-bodied walking birds of treeless plains. All birds of ancient lineage, they may be losing the fight for survival.

The shore birds, gulls and auks form another order, also united because of internal anatomical similarities. The birds of this multifarious assemblage numbering nearly 300 species are highly gregarious and are to be found more widely throughout the world than any other group. The shore birds are small to medium-sized waders that flock along the margins of waterways and the ocean. The gulls and terns are graceful aerialists. Auks fit the same niche in northern seas that penguins do in the Southern Hemisphere, but have not lost their power of flight. Indeed, they have double-purpose wings which enable them to fly through the air and under the water as well.

Four fifths of the world's living birds are made up of the various orders of land birds, which seem to have had their greatest development in recent geological time. The worldwide pigeons, for example, and the Old World sandgrouse, with their small-headed, short-legged look, total more than 300 living species. They are the only birds able to suck up water when drinking; all other species have to tip their heads up to let the water flow down their throats.

The gaudy parrots, which come in all the colors of the rainbow, are bigheaded with deep, hooked beaks and dexterous, prehensile feet. Living for the most part throughout the tropics, they number 317 living species. Not far removed from them anatomically but quite different in shape are the worldwide cuckoos and the touracos of Africa, slim-bodied birds with long tails. Their feet, with two toes forward and two aft, as in the parrots, are weaker and lacking in dexterity. If we lump the cuckoos and touracos the order numbers 143 species.

Owls were once classified with the hawks because of their hooked beaks and curved talons, but they are actually unrelated to those predatory birds. Rather they furnish another good example of convergent evolution, birds of separate origin developing similar features because of their way of life. Owls take over the night shift from the day-flying hawks and are best characterized by their loose feathering, large heads and large, forward-facing eyes framed by round facial disks. Nearly worldwide, they number 132 species.

Another order of nocturnal birds, the goatsuckers, possess fluffy owl-like plumage, but their beaks and feet have degenerated into insignificance. They are flying insect traps, capturing their quarry in cavernous gaping mouths. The whippoorwill and the nighthawk are the best-known North American examples of this group, which numbers 92 species.

The most aerial of birds are the swifts, saber-winged, swallowlike birds that spend all their active hours in the open sky. As in the goatsuckers, beaks and feet have atrophied to near uselessness. Most systematists lump the swifts in

THE LONG AND THE SHORT OF HUMMINGBIRD BILLS

Although nobody knows what the earliest hummingbird bills were like, experts suspect that their dimensions were generally much the same as the bill of the hermit, since most modern hummingbirds' bills are similar to it. However, others have diverged in remarkable ways. The sicklebill's has the most extreme curve of any species, the thornbill's is the shortest, and the swordbill's, at five inches, is the longest. Each is especially adapted for feeding from flowers of a particular size and shape.

HERMIT

SICKLEBILL

THORNBILL

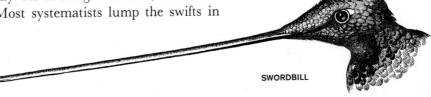

SWORDBILL

15

HOW THE WHITE TERN
GETS ITS NAME

Classification is the sorting out of the different kinds of plants and animals into increasingly narrow categories: kingdom, phylum, class, order, family, genus and species. This process, which gives a special scientific name to every living thing, has many uses. For example, the bird on the cover of this book is sometimes called the white tern and sometimes the fairy tern in English. In other languages it has other names. But its scientific name, "Gygis alba," is an unmistakable label the world over and eliminates all confusion. Here is how the white tern is classified and its name derived:

KINGDOM: ANIMAL *(as distinct from plant)*

PHYLUM: CHORDATA *(animals with a dorsal supporting rod, the notochord. In most adult chordates, it is replaced by a backbone; these are the vertebrates)*

CLASS AVES *(Latin for birds. Excludes other vertebrates like mammals and fishes)*

ORDER: CHARADRIIFORMES *(from a Greek word meaning birds that live in ravines or cliffs. Includes gulls, terns, auks, plovers)*

FAMILY: LARIDAE *(from the Greek word for gull. Includes gulls and terns)*

GENUS: GYGIS *(from the Greek for water bird. Includes one group of terns only)*

SPECIES: (GYGIS) ALBA *(from the Latin for white)*

In short: "Gygis alba," the white tern, with only the generic and specific names being used for its designation.

the same order as the hummingbirds, pointing out that they branched off the same stem. The gemlike, needle-billed hummers, which include the tiniest of all birds, number perhaps 320 species and are all found in the New World. No Old World group has ever become as efficient at the delicate art of nectar feeding.

The layman is puzzled when he reviews the orders of birds. Why are ostriches, rheas and emus put into separate orders when they look so much alike? And why are loons and grebes in separate orders—or hawks and owls? On the other hand, birds as dissimilar as sandpipers and puffins are placed in the same order. So are cranes and coots. All of this becomes even more puzzling when one looks at the orders of land birds.

Systematists find that the superficial appearance of birds may be deceiving. Unrelated birds may look similar because of a similar way of life—evolution has decreed it so, and they have converged. On the other hand, birds may look very different yet have come from the same ancestral stock; they have diverged. For this reason, students are more likely to base their decisions as to the major groups on such points of internal anatomy as the skeleton, the musculature, the palate structure or the anatomy of the foot—characteristics that indicate more accurately their common ancestry.

Thus the colies, or mousebirds, a small group of six African birds with crests and slender tails, have been put in an order of their own, based partly on their curious foot structure. So have the brightly colored tropical trogons, which are among the world's most beautiful birds.

The kingfishers and their allies are another great order of fantastic variety, classified by their peculiar feet, which are "syndactyl," having the front toes joined for part of their length. The kingfishers with their spearlike bills are nearly worldwide. Other gaudily colored families belonging to this order are the tiny, chubby todies of the West Indies; the motmots of the American tropics that pluck the barbs of their own tail feathers so that the tips look like tennis rackets; the handsome bee eaters, the rollers and the hoopoes of the Old World; and the huge, bizarre hornbills of the Old World tropics. All 192 species nest in holes, usually in banks of earth or in trees.

The woodpeckers and their allies, numbering 377 species, are also hole nesters and include such dissimilar families as the barbets with their whiskery bills, the iridescent jacamars and huge-billed toucans. The toucans make up for the lack of hornbills in the New World tropics.

Condensed as this brief review has been, it still gives an idea of the great variety of the orders. None, however, can compare with the passerines, or perching birds. This order is by far the largest; it contains just about 5,110 species, which have been divided into about 55 families. They range in size and beauty from tiny wrens to large, gorgeous birds of paradise and lyrebirds. This galaxy, three fifths of all the world's birds, has developed most strongly in relatively recent times. In an epoch when such ancient types as the ostriches, pelicans, cranes and others are on the way out, the passerines may well inherit the earth, or that fragment of it that man spares for them.

Although many systematists today regard the finches and sparrows as the most "evolved" of all the perching birds, the older ornithologists put the crows and jays at the top of the family tree. Perhaps they were right; certainly these resourceful birds are plastic, relatively unspecialized, opportunistic and probably capable of much further evolution—and that is what counts.

THE HORNED GREBE, A LOBE-FOOTED MARSH DWELLER, BELONGS TO A PRIMITIVE BIRD ORDER LITTLE CHANGED IN SOME 80,000,000 YEARS

The Living Birds

Descended 140 million years ago from reptilian stock similar to that which produced the dinosaurs, birds have radiated explosively over the earth. They show a wide variety of sizes, shapes, colors, and habits. They live in every continent and occupy almost every conceivable niche. Some even nest underground. All together there are 8,580 living species, plus a few dozen yet to be discovered.

Piciformes
Red-breasted Toucan

Trogoniformes
Quetzal

Columbiformes
Pintail Green
Pigeon

Strigiformes
Spectacled Owl

Struthioniformes
Ostrich

Rheiformes
Rhea

Anseriformes
Mandarin Duck

Apterygiformes
Kiwi

Casuariiformes
Australian Cassowary

Galliformes
Golden Pheasant

Sphenisciformes
Rockhopper Penguin

Tinamiformes
Crested Tinamou

Charadriiformes
Pheasant-tailed Jacana

The
27 Orders
of Birds

(One Representative from Each)

Apodiformes
Streamertail

Passeriformes
Red Bird of Paradise

Coliiformes
White-headed Mousebird

Psittaciformes
Gold and Blue Macaw

Coraciiformes
Lilac-breasted Roller

Procellariiformes
Black-browed Albatross

Cuculiformes
Red-crested Touraco

Caprimulgiformes
Pennant-winged Nightjar

Ciconiiformes
Glossy Ibis

Pelecaniformes
Brown Pelican

Gruiformes
Demoiselle Crane

Falconiformes
White-headed Vulture

Podicipediformes
Great Crested Grebe

Gaviiformes
Arctic Loon

Roger Tory Peterson

The 27 Orders

Every one of the 8,580 living species of birds has been assigned by ornithologists to one of 27 major groups or orders, although some experts put the number at 29, placing flamingos and touracos into orders of their own. Many of the birds in a single order may seem wildly unrelated, but they have skeletal or other features which, to trained scientific eyes, relate them unmistakably. The list below opens with the most primitive orders and ends with the most advanced. The figures for families and species are the latest available and conform to those in *The World of Birds* by James Fisher and Roger Tory Peterson (Doubleday, 1964). They show dramatically how poorly the more primitive orders are managing to survive compared to more highly evolved ones.

ORDER	LIVING FAMILIES	LIVING SPECIES
Sphenisciformes: penguins	1	15
Struthioniformes: ostriches	1	1
Casuariiformes: cassowaries, emus	2	4
Apterygiformes: kiwis	1	3
Rheiformes: rheas	1	2
Tinamiformes: tinamous	1	42
Gaviiformes: loons	1	4
Podicipediformes: grebes	1	17
Procellariiformes: albatrosses, fulmars, petrels	4	81
Pelecaniformes: tropic birds, pelicans, boobies, cormorants, anhingas, frigate birds	6	50
Ciconiiformes: herons, storks, flamingos, etc.	6	117
Anseriformes: screamers, swans, geese, ducks	2	149
Falconiformes: vultures, hawks, eagles, etc.	5	274
Galliformes: grouse, quails, turkeys, etc.	7	250
Gruiformes: cranes, rails, coots, bustards, etc.	12	185
Charadriiformes: jacanas, plovers, sandpipers, stilts, gulls, terns, auks, etc.	16	293
Columbiformes: sandgrouse, pigeons	2	301
Psittaciformes: parrots, parakeets, cockatoos, lories, lorikeets, macaws, lovebirds	1	317
Cuculiformes: touracos, cuckoos	2	143
Strigiformes: owls	2	132
Caprimulgiformes: frogmouths, nightjars	5	92
Apodiformes: swifts, hummingbirds	3	388
Coliiformes: mousebirds	1	6
Trogoniformes: trogons	1	35
Coraciiformes: kingfishers, todies, motmots, bee eaters, rollers, hoopoes, hornbills	10	192
Piciformes: barbets, honey guides, puffbirds, jacamars, toucans, woodpeckers	6	377
Passeriformes: flycatchers, larks, swallows, wrens, thrushes, warblers, sparrows, etc.	55	5,110
TOTALS	155	8,580

Red-footed Booby

One of the Pelecaniformes, an ancient order of fisheaters that includes the pelicans and cormorants, this bird nests on bushes and shows little fear of man. It has the long beak, large wings and short legs of the order, as well as webs between all four toes of each foot—the group's unique feature.

Mute Swan

Rearing in the water, a mute swan shows the pointed wing tips, dense plumage and broad, flat bill of the Anseriformes— the swans, geese, ducks and relatives. A wild European species brought to America as an ornamental park bird, it has spread widely in the northeastern states.

American Goshawk

This skillful predator, built for quick maneuvering, takes grouse and rabbits. Like most other Falconiformes— the hawks and eagles—it has strong wings, a hooked bill, sharp talons and keen eyesight. The carrion-eating vultures also belong to this order but lack the clutching talons.

Red Jungle Fowl

The progenitor of all domestic chickens, the red jungle fowl of Southeast Asia is grouped with such other fowl-like birds as grouse, pheasants and turkeys in the order of Galliformes. These are scratching birds, with strong feet and breast meat that is, as man well knows, white and succulent.

European Coot   A marsh bird, the European coot has lobed toes that work like
rubber fins when it swims. Coots are related to cranes,
rails and their allies, and classified as Gruiformes. This
order shows wide diversity but has recently lost—
and is losing—more species than any other major order.

Royal Tern   Erupting from a South Carolina colony, royal terns fill the sky with flailing wings. Terns are closely related to the gulls and black skimmers and belong with them to the order Charadriiformes, along with auks, puffins, skuas and a host of wading shore birds ranging from sandpipers and plovers to

stately avocets. Its members are found throughout
the world, even including the arctic and the edge of Antarctica.
The Charadriiformes are traditionally associated with the sea,
beaches, marshes and salt meadows, but many of them are
found inland, hundreds of miles from the ocean. Most of them
are strong fliers, and some are the most remarkable migrators
known. The golden plover, which is about the size of
a robin and does not light on the water to rest, can
nevertheless fly nonstop 2,400 miles from eastern Canada to
South America and arrives with only a two-ounce weight loss.

Victoria Crowned Pigeon

One of the biggest pigeons, this 26-inch crested
species belongs to the order Columbiformes,
to which the extinct dodo also belonged.
The Columbiformes drink by sucking up water,
instead of tilting their heads back to swallow.

Rainbow Lorikeet

Brilliant plumage, a hooked beak and
a distinctive toe arrangement—two in front
and two in back—place the rainbow lorikeet among
the ranks of such birds as parrots,
macaws and budgerigars in the Psittaciformes.

Donaldson's Touraco

Though African touracos are classified with cuckoos
as Cuculiformes, recent research suggests that they may
be more related to the fowl-like birds. Some
ornithologists would put them in a new order with
the South American hoatzins, now in the Galliformes.

Hoopoe

A long-beaked male hoopoe brings a meal to its waiting family. Like such other Coraciiformes as kingfishers, hornbills and bee eaters, hoopoes nest in cavities. Possibly because of their foul nesting habits and the fact that a musty odor exudes from the female's preen gland, hoopoes, whose flesh is edible, are among the proscribed foods of the Old Testament.

Tawny Frogmouth

Nocturnal, as are most of the Caprimulgiformes, the tawny frogmouth has its own method of catching insects: eschewing flying prey it flutters down on creeping things. This order also contains the insect-catching potoos, nightjars, whippoorwills, nighthawks and the noninsectivorous oilbird.

Starling   The aggressive, extremely adaptable common starling, shown here in white-tipped fall plumage, is but one of 5,110 species in the Passeriformes, the biggest and perhaps most highly evolved of the 27 bird orders. The passerines, or perching birds, got started only 60 million years ago, in

contrast to the waterfowl, which go back 115 million years, and they are found on every continent except one—Antarctica. They are land birds, small to medium in size, with the raven and lyrebird among the largest. Because of their recent, rapid radiation, the differences between the families tend to be less well defined than those in other orders and thus a family tree is more difficult to draw. European ornithologists usually place the intelligent crows and jays on the uppermost branch, but most American experts give top place to such seedeaters as the sparrows and the finches.

2

What It Takes to Fly

Mᴏʀᴇ than anything else, the feather is responsible for the fact that birds can fly. Flight itself is not unique among animals—most insects fly and one family of mammals, the bats, has developed true flight. Even man, through that extension of himself, the machine, now flies. But the feather is unique and has enabled birds to become unquestionably the most efficient aeronauts of all.

The feather is a marvel of natural engineering. It is at once extremely light and structurally strong, much more versatile than the stretched skin on which a bat supports itself in flight or the rigid structure of an aircraft's wing—and far more readily repaired or replaced when damaged.

Examine the cut-off quill feather of a pigeon. Though nearly weightless it has strength. The stiff shaft of the quill provides rigidity where support is needed, yet it is supple toward its tip, where flexibility is required for split-second aerial maneuvering. Feel the sleekness of the web, soft yet firm. Separate the barbs; zipper them together again by running them through the fingertips as a bird would preen with its bill. The intricacy of the design that allows this can be appreciated by putting the feather under a microscope. It will be seen that each parallel barb, slanting diagonally from the shaft, is not hairlike, but appears as a

FEATHERS FOR FLYING

SHAFT

BARB

A bird's flight feather consists of a central shaft with a series of parallel barbs extending diagonally out from it on each side. The barbs in turn have smaller filaments sticking out from them. Equipped with hooks, these tiny filaments lock into a mesh, providing the flight surface that the bird needs to push against the air.

miniature replica of the feather itself, with numerous smaller side branches, or barbules, that overlap those of the neighboring barbs in a herringbone pattern. These in turn have tiny projections called barbicels, many of which are equipped with minute hooks that neatly hold everything in place. The single pigeon feather under scrutiny may have several hundred thousand barbules and millions of barbicels and hooklets.

How did this structural marvel evolve? It takes no great stretch of imagination to envisage a feather as a modified scale, basically like that of a reptile—a longish scale loosely attached, whose outer edges frayed and spread out until it evolved into the highly complex structure that it is today. In fact, birds still wear scales very much like those of reptiles on their feet and legs. And today the scales on the bare shanks of the bald eagle develop from germ buds quite like those which produce the feathers adorning the shanks of the golden eagle. Both are products of the skin, hornified growths as devoid of feeling as our hair or our nails.

The contour feathers are those which give the bird its outward form. Each is built up of a shaft flanked on each side by a web or vane. Clustered around the bases of the contour feathers are the filoplumes, weak, hairlike shafts with a tuft of short barbs at the tip. These are the "hairs" that the housewife singes from a plucked chicken. On many birds there are also down feathers, soft shaftless tufts hidden beneath the sheath of contour feathers. A fourth type, the powder-down feathers, are found in a few groups of birds. Constantly disintegrating into a fine powder, they are used by herons and bitterns to dress their plumage.

It is obvious that feathers contribute more than the gift of flight to birds. As an extremely light, tough, durable padding they also protect the bird's thin and sensitive skin and act as an efficient air conditioner, trapping body heat in the spaces between the fluffed feathers when the temperature is cold, transmitting it through flatly pressed feathers to the outside when it is warm. Nor must we forget the less obvious functions of feathers in the form of crests, beards, plumes and other avian haberdashery.

How many feathers has a bird? It is an old poser—but actually the contour feathers on a bird have been counted many times. A basic rule seems to be, not surprisingly, that the larger the bird the more numerous its feathers. A dairyman, to settle an argument, once counted all the feathers on a Plymouth Rock hen. There were 8,325. Another investigator, patiently plucking a whistling swan, amassed a record of 25,216 feathers, 80 per cent of which came from the head and the extremely long neck. A ruby-throated hummingbird examined by Alexander Wetmore of the Smithsonian Institution showed a low count of 940, yet the tiny bird had many more feathers per unit of body surface than did the swan. Songbirds run between 1,100 and 4,600 feathers, depending on the species, and the counts are remarkably consistent for any one species, although there is often a seasonal difference. Three house sparrows, for instance, taken in winter, averaged somewhat more than 3,550 feathers, whereas two July specimens, in lighter summer garb, had about 400 fewer apiece. A goldfinch may have as many as 1,000 more feathers on its body in winter than it has in summer.

A structure as intricate as a feather, tough though it may be, is not immune to wear. It frays and may even break. Therefore every grown bird must renew its cloak completely at least once a year, usually in late summer after the nesting season. Many birds also have a second complete or partial molt in the spring before the nesting season begins, when they may acquire the full finery which plays a part in aggressive display and courtship.

Feathers are not shed simultaneously, except in penguins. Nor is it a random process. Flight feathers and tail feathers are usually discarded in pairs, one from the right side and its opposite number on the left while the replacements emerge. The bird may lack the support of some of its flight feathers while molting but it is never inhibited in flying. Only ducks, geese and certain other water birds that are not so dependent on their wings for getting food are ever fully deprived of flight in the molting period.

AFTER birds branched off from the reptilian family tree most of the modifications in their skeletal structure became directed toward the airborne life. Their bones became hollow, like dry macaroni, and some of the larger bones even evolved internal struts for reinforcement. Since flight demands a rigid air frame, the body box—the rib case and especially the backbone—became rigid, with some of the bones fused. Only the many-vertebraed neck and tail remained flexible. A keel developed on the breastbone for the attachment of the enormous flight muscles which may account for 15 to 25 per cent of a bird's weight, or even 30 per cent in the case of some hummingbirds. The pectoral muscles of a human, by comparison, weigh less than 1 per cent of his total weight.

Lightness is essential to flight. Not only does a bird have a pair of lungs, small and pink, that lie against the ribs, but also a marvelous system of air sacs that extend in a most intricate way into almost every important part of the body and even lead to air spaces in some of the hollow bones. These delicate sacs with the texture of bubbles enable a bird to use the air it breathes much more efficiently than even a mammal with its relatively larger lungs. The air sacs also act as a thermostatic device, for birds with their rapid metabolism and high body temperatures have no cooling sweat glands.

Superb eyesight is another of the prerequisites of flight. Certainly no other living things can match the visual acuity of birds. A vulture soaring a mile above the earth patiently looking for carrion, a hawk cruising over a meadow in search of a mouse, a warbler gleaning insect eggs under the leaves or a loon in pursuit of its underwater prey—all are endowed with extraordinary vision, far sharper than man's. A sparrow hawk searching out its prey can bring to bear eyes eight times as acute as a man's.

The eye of a bird is extremely large by mammalian standards. The exposed cornea, the only visible part, is small in comparison to the huge eyeball that rests almost immovably in its bony socket. In most birds the eyes actually bulk larger than the brain. The eye of an eagle or a large owl may be as large as a man's, and the eyeball of an ostrich measures two inches across, nearly the diameter of a tennis ball.

Not only can birds see distant things with a greater clarity than we do, but they can also see more clearly at much closer range. A warbler, constantly on the alert for distant danger in the form of a hawk, can instantly bring its focus to bear on the most minute insect egg an inch from its beak, activating strong ciliary muscles which squeeze the rather flat lens into a more spherical shape for close-up vision.

In addition to having a built-in telescope and magnifying glass in the same instrument, most birds are also favored with both monocular and binocular vision. Unlike ours, their eyes are not on the same plane in front (except in owls), but on each side of the head. This gives each eye a great field of monocular vision

THE HAWK'S KEEN EYE

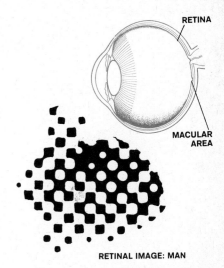

RETINA

MACULAR AREA

RETINAL IMAGE: MAN

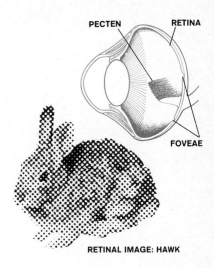

PECTEN   RETINA

FOVEAE

RETINAL IMAGE: HAWK

Hawks see better than men, not because they have "telescopic" vision, as some people think, but because the retinas of their eyes are more densely packed with visual cells—as many as 1.5 million at their most sensitive points, the foveae. The corresponding spot in a man's eye, the macular area, has only 200,000 such cells. This gives the hawk about an eight-to-one advantage, illustrated here by two pictures of a rabbit—one simulating how a small, distant image is crudely received by the retina of a man's eye and the other showing how it is screened in much greater detail by the hawk's keen eye. Man sees the rabbit only as a blur, but to the hawk, the animal is instantly and easily recognizable.

The pecten, a pleated object that furnishes extra blood to the hawk's eye, may also cast shadows on the retina, which helps the bird detect movements at a distance.

35

VISUAL ADAPTATIONS

In nearly all birds some degree of overlap occurs between each eye's field of vision. The area of binocular sight (color) allows depth of field, necessary to judge distance.

OWL

With both eyes facing forward in a relatively flat face, owls have a wider range of binocular vision than any other bird. Binocular sight is vital to hawks and owls because they hunt lively prey. To see to the side or rear, they just turn their heads.

SPARROW

Songbirds like this white-crowned sparrow have eyes set more to the sides of their heads. They feed on seeds and insects and need some forward binocular vision, but they must at the same time be able to see far to the side to avoid predators.

WOODCOCK

The woodcock needs little forward binocular vision since it feeds by probing in the mud with a flexible bill. Its eyes are set far to the rear, enabling it to see in a complete circle without moving its head and providing some overlap to the rear.

to the side. A robin cocking its head as it pauses on the lawn is not "listening" for a worm; it is bringing the area of the most acute vision to bear on that side, the better to detect the movement or glint of a worm at the grass roots.

Straight ahead, where the two monocular fields of vision overlap to form a single image, birds also have a field of binocular vision. Optically they thus have the best of two worlds. The woodcock, however, with its long flexible-tipped bill, has little need for binocular vision in front while probing with its sensitive bill for unseen worms; its problem is to spot danger from behind or above while its bill is in the grip of the soil. For this reason its eyes are placed a bit farther back and a bit higher than those of other birds, resulting in binocular vision to the rear and above as well as a relatively narrow binocular field to the front. It can, in truth, "see from the back of its head" and enjoys a full 360° of vision. So does a duck, although it apparently has a narrower field of binocular overlap behind.

The large eyes of owls, placed on the front of the face like those of man, are primarily binocular. Designed for hunting at dusk or in the dark, these wondrous lenses, not set in flattened eyeballs as in most other birds but in deep horny tubes, might be compared to big, wide-apertured lenses mounted on miniature cameras with a relatively small film surface. If the retina, or "film surface," were in the same proportion to the huge lenses as it is in other birds, there would not be room enough to accommodate the eyeballs.

Their restricted view to the side makes some small owls very easy to capture. The little saw-whet owl, for instance, is caught quite easily by wiggling one's fingers three feet before its face to fix its attention, the while slyly grabbing the bird from behind with the other hand.

Owls not only lack the sweep of monocular vision that most birds have, but their eyes are even more nearly immovably fitted in their sockets. This rigid eye structure is compensated for by quick reflex neck movements and very flexible vertebrae. Unable to see out of the corners of their eyes, owls are constantly moving their heads, and can turn them more than a half circle in either direction. This neck-twisting habit often creates the illusion of turning a full circle, and accounts for the ancient superstition that owls can be made to wring their own necks. Many a boy has tried to do this by walking around and around an owl's roosting tree. But when the halfway point is reached, quick as a wink, the head pivots back to the other side, resuming its steadfast stare. And speaking of winking, owls are the only birds that drop the upper lid when blinking, which makes them look astonishingly human. But when they sleep they raise the lower lid as other birds do. All birds also have a third eyelid, the nictitans, a transparent membrane which, by blinking, keeps the eye moist and at the same time allows them to see.

THE bird with perhaps the most myopic vision is the flightless kiwi of New Zealand, which hunts for worms in the dark, apparently by smell. With its nostrils so conveniently located at the tip of its long, thin bill, the kiwi has little need for eyes, and experiments with buckets of sand have shown that this flightless roly-poly can effectively sniff out its food, quickly digging into those pails in which worms were buried and ignoring the others.

Biologists are not in agreement as to whether smell is of much importance to most birds. The tube-noses (albatrosses, petrels and shearwaters) certainly have a very good sense of taste, if they don't have a fine sense of smell. Ducks are believed to have a good sense of smell. However, ornithologists still argue whether vultures find carrion by sight or by its odor. In 1835 Audubon and John Bachman experimented by hiding some putrid carcasses and exposing others—from the results they concluded that these dark-winged undertakers are guided by sight alone. Nearly a century later, Frank M. Chapman challenged this. At Barro Colorado Island in the Panama Canal he first hid dead mammals in a shed and under burlap. As soon as the carcasses had decayed enough to produce a strong odor, turkey vultures were attracted to the spot and found them. Some critics, not convinced, pointed out that flies and other insects might have betrayed the concealed carcasses. However, when decaying fish with an equally strong odor was hidden, no birds appeared. Chapman concluded that they may have been attracted by one kind of odor and not by another. They were, he thought, finding their food not only by sight, but also by a discriminating use of smell. Kenneth Stager, Curator of Birds at the Los Angeles County Museum, has subsequently discovered that the area of the brain controlling the sense of smell is three times larger in the turkey vulture than the black vulture, strengthening the conjecture that some vultures may, in fact, have better senses of smell than others.

T HE head of a bird, divested of its feathers and skin, seems to be all beak and eyeballs. For the sake of lightness, the bones that make up the skull are fragile, the brain case is small, teeth have been sacrificed. But the beak is important, for it must act as a hand; with it the bird catches things, picks things up and manipulates them in a most expert manner. It may also act as a tool—a hammer or chisel, pincers, tweezers, pruning shears, nutcracker, hook, spear, strainer or even (in pelicans) a market basket. With their beaks birds also dress their plumage, communicate, weave their nests, minister to the needs of their young, kill their prey and defend themselves. It is as though they did all these things with their lips, for that is roughly what beaks are—modified lips, hardened epidermis, forming a horny sheath over the bony projections of the jaws.

In most birds the bill is beautifully designed for its specific job. Consider the efficient meat-tearing hook of a hawk, the elaborate mud-straining apparatus of a flamingo or a spoonbill, the sensitive probing bill of a woodcock, the powerful seed-cracking pincers of a parrot. By contrast, there are the grotesque beaks of the tropical toucans and hornbills, huge and colorful, seemingly so unwieldy that one marvels that the birds can sustain them in flight. Actually, they are almost as light as sponge rubber, honeycombed with air chambers. But just what the survival value is of these exaggerated adornments we do not know.

The bills of birds may be a clue to their relationships, but not always. Herons, terns, loons and kingfishers, for instance, all have similar spearlike bills, though they are not even remotely related. But they do all spend their lives catching fish, and their bills are another example of convergence. Utterly dissimilar, on the other hand, were the bills of the male and female black huia of New Zealand, a wattled, crowlike bird. The male had a stout straight bill for chiseling into dead wood; the female a slender curved bill for extracting the grubs. Together they hunted on the forest floor in a perfect cooperative relationship, unique among birds. Or was it perfect? Perhaps not, for the huia is now extinct.

The feet of birds are as diverse as their bills. Running, perching, wading, scratching and grasping are but some of the more obvious functions of avian feet. Herons have a toothed comb on the center toe with which to scratch themselves and preen. Their slender, widely spaced toes keep them from sinking too deeply into the soft muck; but no heron can match the grotesque length of a

TOE-LOCKING MECHANISM

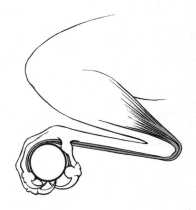

The bulky muscles of a bird's upper leg are attached to tendons (color) running the length of the lower leg and extending to the ends of the toes. When the bird stands or walks on the ground, these tendons are relaxed (above) and the toes spread out. A bird perching on a branch, however, ordinarily squats and bends its legs (below). This pulls the tendons taut over the joints and draws in the long, slender toes, which become so tightly locked that it can sleep without falling off its perch.

FUNCTION FORMS THE FOOT

OSPREY

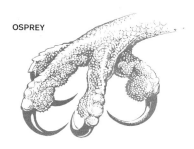

This is a typical predator's foot, better for gripping than for walking. The talons tighten reflexively when grasping prey.

WOODPECKER

To help them hold on as they peck at trees, these birds have two toes at the back to act as braces. Most birds have only one.

MALLARD DUCK

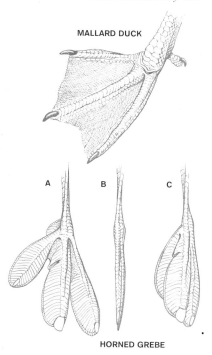

A   B   C

HORNED GREBE

Here are two kinds of feet for swimming. The mallard's foot (top) is webbed. The grebe (below) has paddlelike toes (A) for pushing against the water. On the return stroke they fold backward (B, front view; C, side view) to minimize friction.

jacana's toes, which enable it to trot lightly over floating lily pads. Larks and pipits, which spend most of their time on the ground, have greatly exaggerated hind toenails which act as braces and keep them from rocking back on their heels when the prairie winds blow. Some of the grouse sprout little appendages on the sides of their toes in the fall of the year and by the time the snow flies they have a very useful set of home-grown snowshoes.

Some birds use their feet as hands. A chickadee cracking a sunflower seed holds it firmly with its foot while it hammers it open. A hawk grips its prey while it tears the flesh away with its beak. Parrots are particularly dexterous, some being right-handed, others left-handed.

Most birds that swim—ducks, geese, loons, cormorants, gannets, gulls and albatrosses—are web-footed, while some, such as coots and phalaropes, have flaps or lobes along the sides of their toes. The grebes, often called hell-divers because of their extraordinary submarine abilities, have the most efficient paddles of all, placed so far back that they seem to sprout from the nearly nonexistent tail. Not only do the toes have wide flanges on each side but even the shanks and the nails are flattened to form propeller blades.

Some birds use their feet for attack or defense. The spurs on domestic fowl and pheasants are well known. A kick from the thick two-toed foot of an enraged ostrich is said to be more potent than that of a horse. But probably the most lethal weapons of all are those of the cassowaries, long, knife-blade nails on their inner toes with which they slash each other in combat.

Just as the bills of swifts have degenerated, so have their feet, which are weak and tiny. Since swifts are all wings and mouth, feet are almost unnecessary in their aerial way of life except when they come home to roost. Whippoorwills, nighthawks, swallows and hummingbirds also have diminutive feet and find it difficult to walk—in fact, hummingbirds find it almost impossible.

THE question is often raised how a perching bird can relax in its sleep without falling off a branch. The answer is that the feet have a built-in locking device: flexor muscles and the tendons that run the full length of the leg and automatically pull the toes into a fist when the bird crouches. The deeply curved "meathooks" of birds of prey operate in much the same way. When a hawk or an owl strikes, its legs bend under the weight of the impact and its talons automatically clutch deep into the vitals of its victim.

At first glance it would appear as though the knee of a bird bends in the opposite direction of ours—backward, not forward. But what most people call the "knee," the visible joint below the feathers, is really the heel. The real knee, the fleshy end of the "drumstick," is concealed by the feathers of the body. So is the entire thighbone, or femur, which is embedded in heavy muscles in a rigid forward-directed position. This distributes the weight in such a way as to give the bird in flight a better center of balance, closer to the powerful flight muscles. The long bare shank of a bird, the tarsometatarsus, is actually the same basic structure which, in humans, is made up of the metatarsal bones which form the arch of the foot. Thus a bird, in our terms, walks on its toes with its heels in the air, in somewhat the same way as we go up on our toes when running to pick up speed.

The shape of a bird's wing is beautifully adapted for flight, thick and blunt along the leading edge, narrower and more bladelike on the trailing edge. Its flat or slightly concave underside and more rounded upper surface act together to create lift in a flow of air. Except when gliding or soaring, however, only the basal half of a bird's wing, the arm part, is used for lift. The tip halves of the wings, the hand part, and especially the long flexible primary feathers, act as propellers and control surfaces. In this respect the design of a bird's wing differs radically from that of an aircraft, whose rotary propellers are not an integral part of the wing. In flapping flight each "propeller" moves in a semicircle—forward on the downward stroke, pulling the bird along, then backward (with negligible motive power) on the upbeat. At the moment of transition between downstroke and upstroke the flexible primary feathers become "slotted" to allow the air to slip through freely. Meanwhile the basal half of the wing continues to exert lift and to stabilize flight. The leading edge may be tilted upward, increasing the angle of attack as the wing meets the air stream, and thereby assuring greater lift.

THOUSANDS of papers have been written on the aerodynamics of bird flight, but a bird's wing with its many flexible moving parts which twist and bend under the pressure of the air, particularly in flapping flight, defies the sort of critical analysis to which we can subject the rigid wing of an aircraft. Wind tunnels, smoke streams and mathematical formulas fail to give us more than an inkling of the answers. Perhaps electronic computers may someday help us define the forces acting on the wing of a bird in flight.

The smaller the bird the faster the wingbeat. A ruby-throated hummingbird may beat its wings at the fantastic rate of 50 to 70 times per second, which puts it within the wingbeat spectrum of sphinx moths and certain other large insects whose buzzy wing motion can be stopped photographically by using stroboscopic light. A mockingbird beats its wings 14 times per second, a pigeon 5 to 8, while a ponderous pelican may flap its huge wings as slowly as 1.3 times per second.

As the ornithologist Crawford Greenewalt has pointed out, when Nature designed the hummingbirds she changed her structural model. Whereas all other birds except swifts articulate their wings freely at the shoulder, elbow and wrist, the hummingbird articulates mainly at the shoulder. The elbow and wrist, though not "frozen," move less freely and the arm bones themselves are extremely short. The long paddlelike wing, which is virtually all hand, rotates at the shoulder very much like the wings of an insect. It may well be that size necessitated this change in wing design and it is perhaps no accident that hummingbirds bridge the gap between birds and insects. Imagine a hummingbird the size and weight of a swan: it has been computed that if its wings were built on the usual hummingbird model, they would have to be 32 feet long!

Whereas most birds suggest conventional aircraft, hummingbirds operate more like helicopters, as ultra-high-speed pictures reveal. Crawford Greenewalt comments: "If a helicopter hovers, the rotor is in a plane parallel to the earth's surface—so are the wings of a hummingbird. As the helicopter moves forward or backward, the rotor tilts in the appropriate direction—so do the wings of a hummingbird. The helicopter can rise directly from a given spot without a runway for take-off—so can a hummingbird."

Hummingbirds are often credited with being the only birds able to fly backward. A downward scoop with the tail and a reversal of the wings which are literally mounted on a swivel allow the tiny bird to back away from a flower before making a fast getaway. Actually, as slow-motion movies show, certain other birds like the flycatchers and warblers can sometimes fly backward for a brief moment.

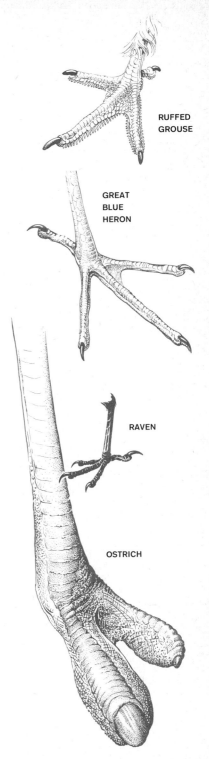

RUFFED GROUSE

GREAT BLUE HERON

RAVEN

OSTRICH

Four different kinds of walking feet are pictured here. The scaly fringes that appear every winter on the feet of the grouse (which does not migrate) help hold it up in snow, while the extra long toes and small webs of the marsh-wading heron keep it from sinking in the mud. The raven's all-purpose foot is suited for perching, walking or scratching. Drawn to scale below is the huge foot of the flightless ostrich. Like many grazing mammals, this grazing bird has only two toes.

Much the simplest form of flight, certainly much less complicated than flapping or hovering, is gliding flight This, as we have seen, was undoubtedly the way the earliest birds flew, dawn creatures such as *Archaeopteryx* which are believed to have clambered up rocks and trees and launched themselves forth on set wings. Swallows employ gliding flight—several strong wing strokes and a glide. So do pelicans traveling in formation, geese coming in for a landing, and many other birds. Gliding saves energy, but gravity and air conditions determine how far a bird can skim before it must flap again.

A much more specialized skill is soaring, which makes use of rising air currents so effectively that for long periods no flapping is required. The hawk watchers who converge by hundreds on Pennsylvania's Hawk Mountain on autumn weekends are often given a great exhibition of soaring flight at its best. If the wind is in the northwest and there is a strong updraft along the windward slope, the birds coast in a straight line along the ridge. An osprey clocked at two points along the ridge traveled 80 miles per hour without flapping its wings. On warm sunny days when the thermals, those "winds that blow straight up," rise from the heated earth, the hawk watchers are treated to a magnificent display of true soaring—red-tailed hawks, turkey vultures and sometimes eagles swinging like sailplanes in wide and graceful circles on the invisible columns of rising air.

Soaring birds, with a large sail surface in proportion to their weight, fall into two very different types: (1) those with broad wings and fanlike tails as exemplified by many of the hawks, eagles and vultures, and (2) those with extremely long but relatively narrow wings, ocean wanderers such as gulls, frigate birds and albatrosses.

A VULTURE or a condor is a vision of effortless majesty as it glides on motionless wings along the face of a cliff, its primaries deeply slotted, like giant fingers, to counteract turbulence and to maintain stability in the uncertain air currents of the cordillera. No airplane would dare to negotiate the narrow canyons; no man-made craft is as maneuverable. Coming in for a landing the great bird first drops its "retractable landing gear"—its feet. Reducing its wing area with a mere shrug of the shoulders it loses altitude, then plunges straight at the ledge, so fast that a crash landing seems unavoidable. But at precisely the right moment it brings the braking action of its wings into play. The cupped wings act as flaps, the tail is lowered and spread, and the bird lands adroitly, its leg action absorbing the impact. For a brief moment it holds its wings high over its body, then neatly folds them in. This magical exhibition of purely physical control makes an airplane seem crude indeed.

The most effortless of all aerialists are the large albatrosses. Their realm is the sea where thermals are few and deflected air currents are ineffective for more than a few feet above the wave tops. However, due to frictional drag, ocean winds are stronger at a height of 50 feet than they are near the sea surface. The wandering albatross, with its wing span of 11 feet or more, exploits this phenomenon in a methodical way. Once it has gained the level of the faster upper wind currents, it uses them to build up speed in a long down-wind glide on set scimitarlike wings. Then, almost brushing the wave crests, it turns into the slower surface winds, its great speed sending it zooming upward again. By thus alternating glide and zoom, the great bird can tack effortlessly over the sea for hours without beating its wings. The stronger the gale, the more it revels in its powers—the most efficient sailplane of them all.

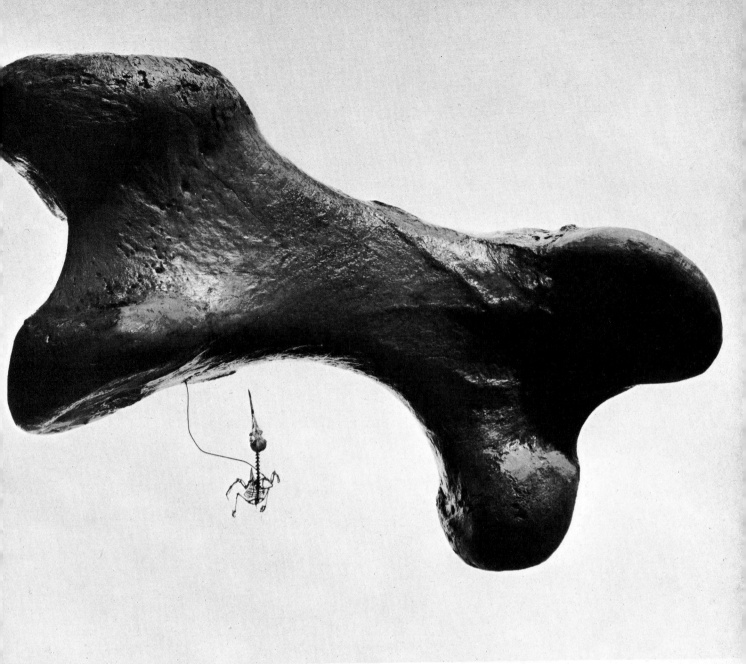

A HUMMINGBIRD'S SKELETON AND THE HOLLOW THIGH BONE OF AN EXTINCT ELEPHANT BIRD SHOW HOW TINY AND HOW BIG BIRDS CAN BE

Built for a World of Air

Birds that fly—from the tiniest hummingbird to the largest alba-tross—are far more alike in their make-up than other groups of animals are. This is because flight has demanded that they have skeletons that are light but strong, muscles that are powerful but not a burden, feathers that conserve heat while providing lift and propulsion, and the sharpest eyes in the entire animal kingdom.

Flying Made Easier

The wing of a bird is constructed on sound aerodynamic principles. Not only is it streamlined to cut through the air with little drag, but it is also curved to produce lift, the force that keeps birds aloft. Air flowing past the leading edge and over the convex upper surface of the wing speeds up and tends to pull

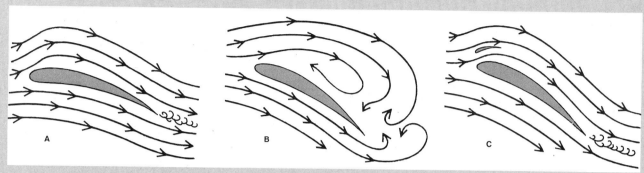

LIFT is increased as the wing is tilted increasingly upward into the air stream. As long as the air flows smoothly, the wing flies (A). But if it is tilted sharply, turbulence sets in above the wing and lift is destroyed (B). On the leading edge of a bird's wing there is a group of feathers, the alula, which keeps the air flow smooth as the wing tilts (C), so that lift is maintained.

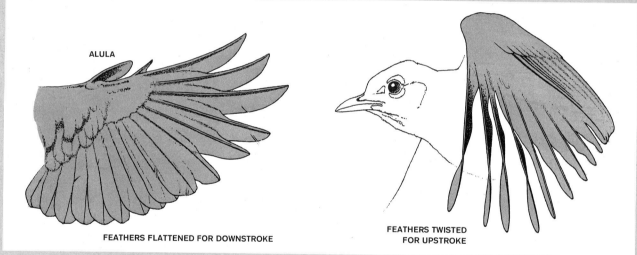

ALULA

FEATHERS FLATTENED FOR DOWNSTROKE

FEATHERS TWISTED FOR UPSTROKE

ON THE DOWNSTROKE, the power stroke in a bird's flight, the primary feathers hold firm, overlapping each other to present a closed surface to the air *(left)*. On the upstroke, however *(right)*, they open to allow air to slip through, making it easier to lift the wing. The alula, shown on the leading edge in the drawing at left, is under muscular control, ready when needed.

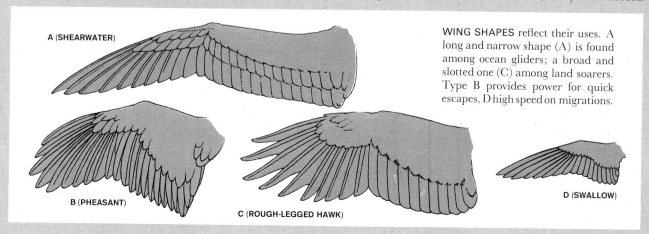

A (SHEARWATER)

B (PHEASANT)

C (ROUGH-LEGGED HAWK)

D (SWALLOW)

WING SHAPES reflect their uses. A long and narrow shape (A) is found among ocean gliders; a broad and slotted one (C) among land soarers. Type B provides power for quick escapes, D high speed on migrations.

away, thus creating a drop in pressure, while pressure on the concave undersurface remains fairly constant. It is the difference in the pressures above and below the wing that creates lift. As in airplanes, slots and flaps may increase or decrease lift. Wings vary among birds, reflecting the adaptations they have made to different niches in their environment. Gulls, dwelling in wide, open spaces, have evolved light, long, narrow wings for soaring on air currents. Pigeons, on the other hand, occupying a more cramped niche in which such currents are less dependable, have short, well-muscled wings which make them power fliers.

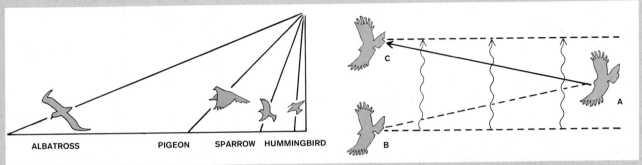

GLIDING ABILITY of birds varies widely. Here, greatly exaggerated vertically, are the distances achieved by four species. The hummingbirds, with tiny wings, can scarcely glide at all.

STATIC SOARING may occur when a broad-winged bird is carried aloft on warm air currents rising faster than the bird can fall. In still air, such a bird would glide from A to B position.

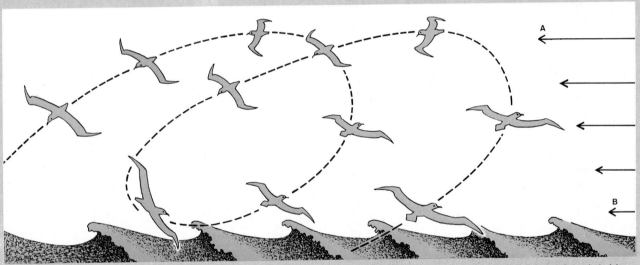

DYNAMIC SOARING permits an albatross to glide for hours over the ocean without flapping its wings. Here an albatross is shown rising against the wind from B level, where the wind is slowed by the friction of the waves, to A level, where it is blowing at a faster rate. Wheeling, the albatross glides downwind, gaining sufficient increased momentum to rise against it again.

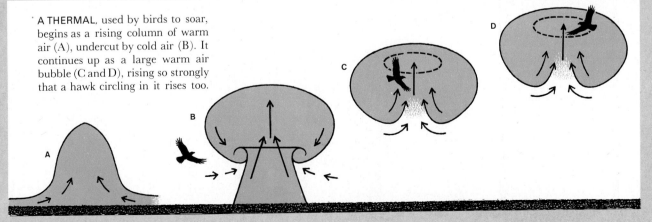

A THERMAL, used by birds to soar, begins as a rising column of warm air (A), undercut by cold air (B). It continues up as a large warm air bubble (C and D), rising so strongly that a hawk circling in it rises too.

The Mechanics of Forward Flight

STRONG FLIERS like ducks do not swim through the air as many people believe; they are actually propeller-driven on the same basic principle as an airplane. In the case of a bird, however, the propellers are at the tips of the wings in the form of the primary feathers. The power is applied on the downstroke (*above, left*). As the wing is pulled down against the resisting air, the tips of the primaries are bent upward and twisted at an angle to the wing as a whole. In this position they bite propeller-

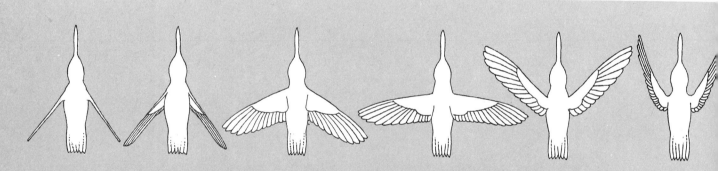

The Mechanics of Hovering Flight

AERIAL ACROBATS, hummingbirds can fly straight up and even backward, but perhaps their most remarkable feat is hovering motionless in the air while sipping nectar from a flower. The secret of this ability lies in a wing structure quite different from that of most other birds. The wing as a whole is almost rigid with little movement at "wrist" and "elbow," and it is attached to the shoulder by a swivel joint. These views, from above and from the side, show how the whole wing acts like a helicopter's

fashion into the air and as they are brought farther and farther down they are impelled forward, pulling the entire wing and hence the bird's body along with them. At the end of the downstroke the wing tips are on a level with the bill. On the

upstroke, the primaries separate to permit easy passage of air; the wing tips move upward and backward against the air, still providing slight propulsion, while the inner part of each wing, close to the shoulder, provides lift. Then the cycle begins again.

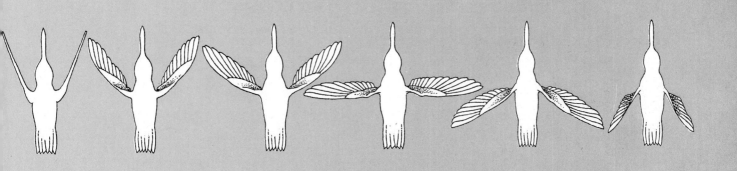

rotor, but sculling back and forth instead of whirling around. On the forward stroke, the wing moves conventionally with the leading edge forward, angled slightly to provide lift but no thrust, as in the first six silhouettes. On the backstroke, the entire

wing swivels almost 180 degrees at the shoulder (next six silhouettes); the leading edge is now turned backward so that on the backstroke the wing achieves the same effect of lift without propulsion. Thus the bird can hang motionless in the air.

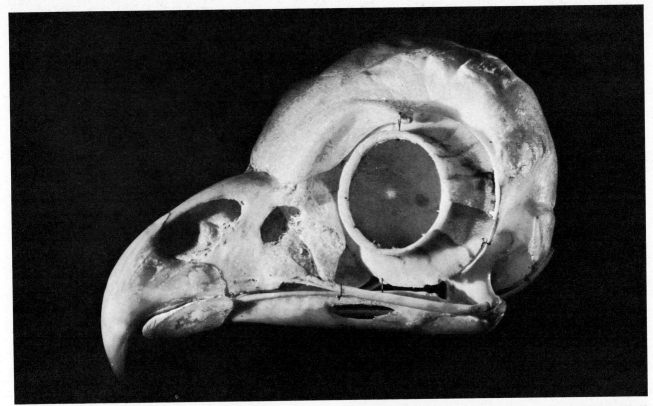

AN OWL'S SKULL SHOWS THE CHARACTERISTIC AVIAN FEATURES OF LARGE EYE SOCKETS AND PAPER-THIN FUSED AND REINFORCED BONES

An Airy Frame

From the inside out, the skeletons of birds are natural marvels of flight engineering and structure. They combine lightness with strength, and in all their parts form beautifully follows function. In all birds that fly, the breastbone, though extremely thin and light, has a deep keel which not only makes it rigid, but, more importantly, provides a large surface for attachment of the powerful flight muscles. Many bones found in other higher vertebrates are missing in the birds, having been discarded in the evolutionary process of lightening the load; others normally jointed are fused for stress-resistance and for further lightness. Most bird bones are hollow and some of these are trussed inside to make them stronger while preserving their flexibility. The skeleton of a three-to-four-pound frigate bird with a seven-foot wingspread may weigh as little as four ounces—less than the weight of the bird's feathers.

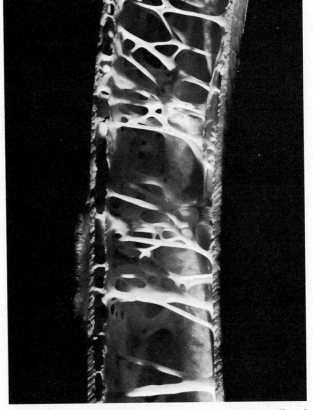

DELICATE IN STRUCTURE, a gull's skeleton, here suspended from its wing, is strongest in the thorax, where reinforced ribs lock onto the breastbone. The spine is semi-fused for rigidity.

A HOLLOW WING BONE, the humerus of an eagle, is stiffened by struts. Air spaces in such bones are often continuations of air sacs in the birds' bodies and may even extend into their toes.

47

AN EGRET, a strong flier, takes off with its long, heavy neck outstretched. Once under way, it will retract the neck into an S and hold its legs stiffly out behind for balance. Because egrets have large wings, which are more efficient than smaller ones, they need flap them only about twice a second, in contrast to the 80 wing beats per second of the tiniest hummingbirds.

A FULL-CHESTED, STUBBY-WINGED BOBWHITE QUAIL ZOOMS WITH A ROCKETING BURST OF ENERGY FROM THE BRUSH WHERE IT WAS HIDING

A Powerful, Air-Cooled Engine

Birds flap their wings with powerful flight muscles which, to use automotive terms, come in two models: one designed to provide explosive bursts of speed for short distances, and another geared for endurance on long hauls. The bobwhite quail above, a ground bird like the chicken, has white flight muscles, quick to contract but meagerly supplied with blood vessels to carry oxygen and other fuel to the fibers and thus incapable of sustained action. For ground birds, flight is strictly a means of escape: if flushed several times, many species become exhausted and may even be picked up in the hand.

By contrast, strong fliers like the egret (*opposite*),
wild ducks, geese and other migrators have red flight muscles, plentifully supplied with blood vessels and not readily tired. Driving the wings, these muscles generate great heat and speed up the body's metabolism. Such heat would be killing were it not regulated by the respiratory system, the most efficient of any in the vertebrates. In addition to a pair of small, bright-red lungs, there are usually at least nine thin-walled air sacs with interconnecting chambers throughout the body. Not only do these bring supplies of oxygen to the tissues for burning, but also, perhaps through the evaporation of water, they help to keep the temperature to a tolerable limit.

49

AN ASIATIC FISHING OWL WINKS WITH A THIRD EYELID. FARSIGHTED OWLS HAVE POOR FOCUSING ABILITY AT CLOSE RANGE AND MUST BACK AWAY

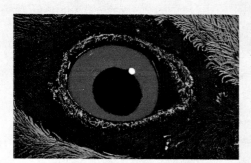

VICTORIA CROWNED PIGEON

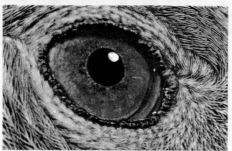

SATIN BOWERBIRD

SOUTHERN GROUND HORNBILL

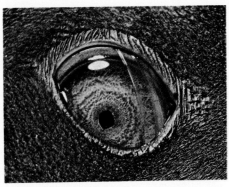
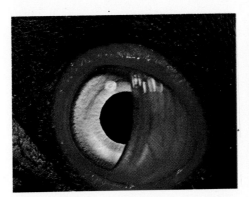

LIKE WINDSHIELD WIPERS, nictitating membranes sweep across the eyeballs of a king vulture and a king penguin. Found in all birds, these transparent third eyelids clean and moisten the cornea. The king penguin can contract its pupil to a square.

Eyes That See Big—and Small

Though they look relatively small, hidden behind their lids and set like gems in protective rings of overlapping bone, birds' eyes are enormous. This is because flight demands that the image be big and all its details sharp. In many birds the eyes must also be able to register and react instantaneously to far objects and near ones—a swift out on patrol for food reacts with incredible speed to the flick of an insect crossing its path just a few inches ahead.

Birds' eyes vary in position and shape from species to species. Most birds have rather flat eyeballs with large retinas for images to play on, excellent for scanning the landscape. Birds of prey have rounder or almost tubular eyes. These take in less territory than flat ones do, but see farther and in greater detail, pinpointing living targets with the precision of a bombsight.

A bird has more sensory cells in its eyes than other animals have, particularly in the area of the fovea, a small depression in the retina at the point of acutest vision. The fovea's convex sides help magnify part of the image—as much as 30 per cent in some bird species. The retinas of hawks are from four to eight times as sensitive as those of humans, making these birds the keenest-sighted of all living things.

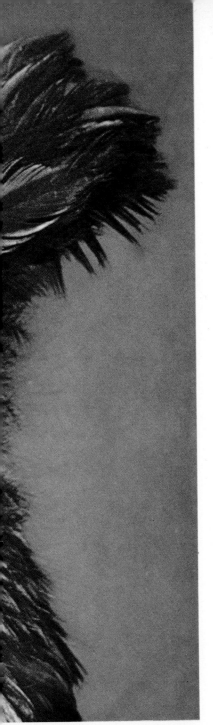

ROM NEAR OBJECTS TO SEE THEM WELL

PALLAS' SEA EAGLE

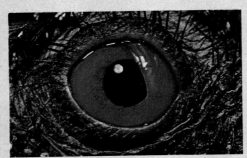

HOATZIN

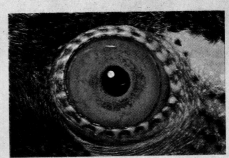

DOUBLE-CRESTED CORMORANT

CONTOUR FEATHER

DOWN FEATHER

FILOPLUME

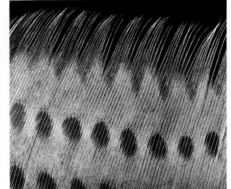

OWL WING FEATHER

The Indispensable Feather

A bird's feathers have to do many things. Not only must they provide lift surfaces for wings and tail, but they must protect the bird against the weather and insulate it against loss of heat. Feathers come in almost infinite variety, but they fall into four main categories. Most numerous are the contour feathers which coat the body, giving it a streamlined shape. A house sparrow wears about 3,500 of these in winter, and they are so efficient at sealing in heat that it can maintain a normal temperature of 106.7° F. without difficulty in below-freezing cold. Lying beneath them are the soft down feathers, also used for insulation. Scattered among both types are the hairlike filoplumes which sometimes protrude from the coat and may serve as a kind of decoration, or possibly as sensory organs. Flight feathers are the long stiff quills found on wings and tail. The webs are of unequal width, with the broader part forming the trailing edge. Among nocturnal owls, flight feathers are equipped with mufflers in the form of comblike projections and fringes for silent attacks on unwary prey.

FLIGHT FEATHER

THE SHIMMERING PLAY OF COLORS in a peacock's feather is caused by refraction and reflection of light from layers of horn that help to keep the true color, brown, from showing through.

A MOLTING TERN FLIES EASILY DESPITE MISSING FEATHERS, WHICH DROP OUT A FEW AT A TIME FROM EACH WING TO MAINTAIN BALANCE

Keeping the Feathers in Shape

Tough though they are, the work that feathers do is tougher still, and to guard against their wearing or falling out prematurely, birds give them constant care. Most birds have oil glands at the bases of their tails, and preen themselves by smearing the oily secretion over their feathers with their beaks. Those which do not secrete oil preen with a powder made up of microscopic particles from feathers so delicate that they are constantly disintegrating into dust.

But even the best-kept feathers deteriorate, and birds must renew their coats at least once a year. Molting generally follows a regular pattern, ranging slowly and symmetrically over the bird, often progressing from rump to head. Ducks, geese and many other water birds shed most of their flight feathers at once and are thus temporarily grounded. At this time male ducks wear a dull coat called the "eclipse plumage." Occasionally all the feathers are shed simultaneously, as in penguins, whose old coat is pushed away by the emergence of new feathers growing from beneath. Because penguins are flightless, a complete molting is no hazard to them, but there are some birds which are made all but helpless by this. During a period of near-nakedness, the female African hornbill must stay in its walled-up nest cavity for safety and rely on the male for food.

FALL MOLTING of the rock ptarmigan helps to camouflage this ground bird of the tundra and alpine slopes by giving it a patchwork appearance. Brown feathers are replaced by white ones.

WINTER PLUMAGE of the ptarmigan is pure white to blend with snow. The spring molting, triggered perhaps by the change in temperature, will produce an almost all-brown summer coat.

TWISTING ITS NECK INTO AN EIGHT, A FLAMINGO GOES ABOUT THE TASK OF ARRANGING AND OILING ITS FEATHERS

UPSIDE-DOWN HEAD of a short-
eared owl shows the extraordinary
flexibility which allows these birds
to swivel their heads in almost every
direction. This one is trying to focus
on a close-up object—the camera.

3

Birds as
Food Gatherers

NEARLY every category of animal and plant life on earth is exploited by some
bird. Even the remains of whales and elephants find their way into the
diets of scavenging gulls and vultures (and so, occasionally, does man himself).
At the other end of the avian food spectrum is one of the most minute of primitive plants, blue-green alga, the main source of subsistence for the 3,000,000 or
more lesser flamingos that crowd the salt lakes of East Africa. In fact, one of
the reasons that flamingos, birds of ancient lineage, still exist at all is because
they can use this environment that few other creatures can exploit.

The varied hosts of birds that live on earth today survive because they have
been able to carve out special niches of their own, either geographically or en-
vironmentally. Although unrelated birds with somewhat different habits may
overlap in their territories, evolution seldom permits closely related species—
two kinds of jays, for example—to occupy the same territory and exploit the
identical niche in the same way.

Every environment except for the truly sterile areas of the world has its specific
birds. They have developed along with the food resources in the various living
places—the forests, mountains, grasslands, scrub, marshes, deserts, tundra,

rivers, lakes, islands and the sea, and lately the cities and farms. The association is not accidental, but is the result of natural selection over long periods of time toward a more successful life.

It has often been claimed that were it not for the birds, insects would inherit the earth. This is clearly an exaggeration, for insects have effective predators and parasites within their own ranks (birds, incidentally, do not discriminate between "pest" insects and "beneficial" insects). But birds do exert great controlling pressures at the critical periods. Warblers and other migrants arrive at precisely the time when myriads of small insect larvae are hatching on emerging leaves. They continue the assault in the succeeding weeks when their hungry young, which may consume nearly their own weight in food daily, make constant demands. A pair of magnolia warblers nesting in a spruce forest in Maine will feed their large young a beakful of insects on an average of once every four minutes. Adult birds, on the other hand, require less fuel. The high water content of caterpillars and other insects may result in an adult insectivorous bird eating 40 per cent of its weight daily, but a seedeater may eat only 10 per cent.

The insects, which have invaded nearly every terrestrial environment on earth, are unable to evade the birds that probe the soil, turn over the leaf litter, search the bark, dig into the trunks of trees, scrutinize every twig and living leaf. The water is no safe refuge, nor is the air, nor the dark of night. There is a bird of some sort to hunt nearly every insect. Warblers and vireos methodically work the leaves while swallows, swifts and other hunters of flying-insect prey spend most of their waking hours on the wing, ranging hundreds of miles daily in their aerial forays.

In tropical America a number of soberly colored ant birds specialize in following the large swarms of army ants, feeding on the many other insects that are flushed up as the army advances over the jungle floor. Similarly, in Africa, many insect-hunting birds take advantage of the grass fires set by native tribesmen to improve the pasturage. Ground hornbills stalk close to the smouldering tussocks while kestrels hover in the smoke and rollers perch nearby. Grazing animals also act as insect-flushing agents, and in East Africa the bustards, cattle egrets, bee eaters and other species live in intimate association with zebras, antelope, and other herd animals.

MANY birds in their search for insects are preoccupied with the trunks of trees. These include the nuthatches, creepers, woodcreepers and even some wood warblers; but none are as well designed for the job as the woodpeckers. These specialized hammerers spend most of their lives in a perpendicular stance, clamped against a trunk or a branch, the stiff tail acting as a brace and the deeply curved claws, two forward, two aft on each foot, clutching the rough bark. The straight beak, hard as a chisel, is driven in triphammer blows by powerful muscles in the head and neck while the thick skull absorbs the shock. When the subterranean workings of a borer are uncovered an extremely long tongue snakes in to hook it on backward-pointing barbs. The woodpeckers, an old family numbering more than 200 living members, probably developed their skill as far back as the Eocene, more than 50,000,000 years ago.

One of the famous Darwin finches of the Galápagos, the woodpecker finch, has ingeniously circumvented the woodpecker's labors to get at wood-boring grubs that it cannot reach with its bill. Picking up a slender twig or a cactus-needle two inches long or so, it deftly pokes it into the hole, much as one would spear a cocktail snack with a toothpick, and out comes the grub. This is believed to be the only bird that actually makes use of a tool to get its food.

In the beginning, all birds probably ate animal food. Seed-eating is almost certainly a later specialization. A suggestive clue is the fact that nearly all seed-eating birds start off their newly hatched young on insects, then gradually make the switch to a vegetable diet. Pigeons, an exception, get around this by feeding their young on a secretion called "pigeon's milk."

The great proliferation of seed-eating birds must have taken place fairly recently in evolutionary history, mostly within the last 13,000,000 years, after the Miocene, when the seed-bearing plants, especially the grasses and sedges, had their great spread. Birds of several orders eat seeds, but it is among the various families of perching birds, the Passeriformes, that we most often find the stout conical bill that is adapted for seed-cracking. It is particularly typical of the finches and the buntings, which many evolutionists consider among the most recently developed families of birds. However, some taxonomists cannot agree as to where some of the finchlike birds should be placed or how many family stocks should be recognized. As we have seen, such highly functional food-getting structures as bills may not always indicate blood ties, but perhaps merely convergence or parallelism of anatomical development—i.e., the habit of seed-cracking develops, through natural selection, a bill that is capable of cracking seeds.

R oots, tubers, grass, leaves, buds, seeds, fruit pulp, nectar, pollen and sap of various plants find their way into the diet of birds. On the other hand very few birds eat fungi, lichens and some of the other more primitive plants.

To those of us who live in the temperate parts of the Northern Hemisphere it comes as a surprise to learn that nearly one-fifth of all the world's birds feed mainly on nectar. A bird watcher in New England is aware that ruby-throated hummingbirds live on nectar and that Baltimore orioles sometimes poke at blossoms and appear to be getting nectar from them, but he finds it difficult to believe that more than 1,600 other species of birds on five continents take part in nectar feeding.

Most of these birds, to be sure, are in the Southern Hemisphere. The hummingbirds, a rainbow-hued galaxy of about 320 species, are the most efficient of all the nectar gatherers by far, hovering before flowers and probing them deftly with needlelike bills. The tiniest hummingbird, the bee hummingbird of Cuba, is only two and one fourth inches long, smaller than some of the sphinx moths these little birds so closely resemble in contour, wing length and wing action.

Small though it is, the amount of energy burned up by a hummer is phenomenal, as the ruby-throated hummingbird shows. If a normal 170-pound man expended energy at the rate of this little bird, he would have to eat, in a single day, 285 pounds of hamburger or double his own weight in potatoes. Crawford Greenewalt cites an even more astonishing statistic: a man expending energy at the rate of a hovering hummingbird would have to evaporate about 100 pounds of perspiration per hour to keep his skin temperature below the boiling point of water!

In spite of their strong powers of flight, the hummingbirds have never bridged the gap between the New World and the Old. However, a large family of Old World birds, the sunbirds (Nectariniidae), numbering more than 100 species, attempts to fill the flower niche. Most sunbirds are not much larger than the general run of hummingbirds and many are as gaudily colored. But they cannot

AFTER A WOODPECKER PECKS

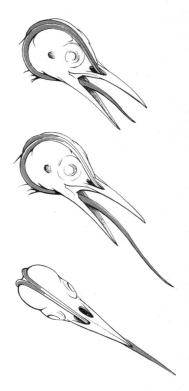

For a woodpecker, chiseling into trees with its bill is only the first step in getting the grubs that live there. It then uses a flexible tongue for penetrating deep into the galleries that wood borers make in trees and snaking out its food. This raises the question: Where does the woodpecker store such a tongue in its small head? Actually, the tongue is rather short. It is part of an apparatus of bones and elastic tissue (shown in color) that goes under the jaw, up around the back of the head and anchors itself in the right nostril, leaving the left one free for breathing. When this apparatus, known as the hyoid, is slid around the head, the tongue is protruded.

A BILL FOR ANY DIET

COCKATOO

The hooked beak of this seedeater is a powerful and efficient nutcracker. After the nut or seed is cracked, the bird picks out the meat with a strong, supple tongue.

CROSSBILL

This scissorslike bill is designed to lever the seeds out of evergreen cones. Other birds must either wait until the cones dry out, or laboriously pick them apart.

OYSTERCATCHER

This bird's bill is higher than it is broad and is inserted like a chisel in partly open oyster shells, paralyzing the occupants before they are able to snap shut.

compare with hummingbirds in their flying skill; they must perch while they sip and only rarely do they hover before a blossom.

Nectar feeders must be flexible to prosper, able to follow the blossoming of the flowers. Hawaiian honey creepers travel in loose flocks from one section of forest on the volcanic slopes to another, their movements dictated by the blooming of the ohia, mamane and other native trees. Hummingbirds in the western United States migrate through the Pacific lowlands when the early spring flowers are at their best, but go up to the high alpine meadows in late summer when the valleys lie parched and brown.

A large branch of the parrot clan, the lorikeets of the Australasian region, specializes in nectar feeding in a crude fashion, crushing the bristly blossoms of eucalypti and other flowering trees and sopping up the sticky juices with their fringe-tipped tongues. Like other parrots, the lorikeets enjoy company and travel the mountain forests in large gangs, concentrating where the blossoms are thickest and signaling noisily to other passing flocks to join them. Twittering and chattering, they pause briefly to decorate a tree with their brilliant colors, then rush away toward new horizons. On Australia's Queensland coast, a beekeeper, Alex Griffiths, has attracted hundreds of rainbow lorikeets with pans of honey to his home in the town of Currumbin. They have accepted his friendship completely, freely perching on his hands, his shoulders and his head. Now the place is a sanctuary and as many as 500 lorikeets come each afternoon to feed on honey and to delight the crowds of human observers who sometimes outnumber the birds.

Tropical fruit-eating birds, like the nectar feeders, are usually gaudily colored and most of them are noisy. Parrots fly in flocks or in twosomes over the tropical forests shrieking loudly. A feeding flock hidden in the foliage below shrieks back, inviting them to share in their good fortune. It is to their mutual advantage that they are gaudy and noisy for in the dark jungle a tree laden with ripening fruit may be far from the next one.

IN marked contrast to them are the soft-voiced waxwings, sleek, crested birds dressed in muted browns and grays. Cedar waxwings may winter as far north as southern Canada but they also go as far south as Panama, traveling in tight flocks and lingering only when they find a treeful of berries. The bird watcher cannot predict their arrivals and departures, for they stay in a neighborhood only as long as the fruit lasts. Thus the well-named Bohemian waxwing will be found in Scandinavia as long as the rowan tree has fruit, but when the berries give out it may cross the North Sea to invade England.

Five sevenths of the surface of the globe is sea. For every square mile of land there are two and a half square miles of salt water and yet the birds that we might properly call sea birds aggregate only about three per cent of the world's species—roughly 260, made up of a dozen families. Some, like most of the gulls and terns, the cormorants, frigate birds and pelicans, stick rather closely to the coasts, so that the truly pelagic birds number less than 150 species.

The sea is rich in life and those birds that have adapted to its quixotic winds and waves and have accepted its harsh terms find a bountiful larder. The oceans are not one uniform ecological block. Planktonic life, the pasturage of the sea, made up of countless minute, floating marine organisms, is not distributed evenly like sugar stirred into a cup of tea; it runs in streaks or ribbons, concentrated by the sea currents and upwellings. Where the organisms are thick the birds assemble.

The colder ocean currents have a far higher density of plankton than warmer areas. This directly affects bird life. Watching from the ship rail in tropical oceans one sees but a tiny fraction of the birds that he would see during the same amount of time in northern or far southern waters. The cold Humboldt Current, for example, flowing northward off the west coast of South America, brings riches to Peru in the form of millions of guanay cormorants, gannetlike piqueros and pelicans which deposit their nitrate-rich guano on the offshore islets. The food cycle of the sea is to be seen here in its most dynamic form. The prevailing southerly winds force the surface water away from the rainless desert coast, allowing colder water to rise from the bottom to take its place. As this water wells upward it brings with it nitrogenous and phosphorous compounds released by the decay of myriads of marine animals and plants. Microscopic algae, tinging the water green, use these nutrients and they in turn are the food base for astronomical numbers of anchovies. Little fish attract bigger fish and birds. No other coastal waters on earth support more sea birds. One oceanographer, Dr. Gerald Posner, recently estimated that "the yearly consumption of fish by guano birds about equals the total annual commercial fisheries catch for the entire United States."

ANHINGA

Also called darters or snakebirds, anhingas impale fish under the water on their spearlike beaks. Long sinuous necks and webbed feet help them in their fishing.

IN the Western Hemisphere, only the Pribilofs in the Bering Sea can match the numbers of sea birds found off the coast of Peru. Here two very similar members of the auk family, the common murre and the thick-billed murre, live side by side on the sea cliffs, along with two species of puffins and two of kittiwake gulls. Biologists wonder: Where is the competition between species here? The two murres seem equally abundant and so do the two puffins. Perhaps each has a different food pattern of which we are not yet aware. As for the two gulls, the red-legged kittiwake is much the scarcer, perhaps a relict species losing out to the more successful black-legged kittiwake.

Although there are roughly 260 birds that we classify as sea birds, there are fully 600 others that we might call water birds—birds of the lakes, shores, estuaries, swamps and marshes. Some of these, like the scoters, eiders, grebes and loons, may even become sea birds for part of the year, or at least birds of the coastal waters.

Loons are among the very few birds with solid, heavy bones. Lack of buoyancy is an asset to a bird that spends most of its time in submarine pursuit of fish. And loons dive far and deep—one was recovered from a fisherman's net 240 feet down. Loons and grebes are both ill-fitted for locomotion on land, so much so that they may avoid taking their feet out of the water (except to fly) for months on end, and finally do so only to clamber onto the nest.

The long-legged "glamour birds," the herons, storks, ibises, spoonbills and cranes, numbering about 120 species, are marshland associates that stalk fish, frogs, small reptiles, crustaceans and large insects. Their stiltlike legs are counterbalanced with equally long necks which make useful periscopes above the marsh grass. Followers of Izaak Walton have often noticed that some of the best fishing is downstream from a heronry. The nitrogenous droppings of the birds enrich the water, fish multiply and the herons exact tribute in return, pointing the way for anglers.

The smaller waders, the snipe, sandpipers, plovers and their relatives, denied access to deeper water, concentrate along the shoreline where they catch sand fleas, probe for marine worms, eat mosquito larvae, take small crabs, or knock limpets off rocks. If it is edible, there is a wader to eat it.

FLAMINGO

Flamingos live on the organic matter found in mud. Their bent bills, fringed at the edges, filter out mud and water and retain the minute plants and animals.

61

Ducks of a feather flock together and although a dozen kinds might consort on a lake or a bay each species has its traditional stopping places. In winter, canvasbacks favor the bay near New York's La Guardia Airport, or the Chesapeake below Baltimore where wild celery grows. Widgeon are grazers and swarm over the golf courses of some west coast cities, while shovelers sift the mud in adjacent ponds. Brant resort to the eelgrass beds of certain salt bays while rafts of scoters dive for mussels in the rougher water off nearby coastal headlands. The mergansers are fish ducks and a thousand rivers and bays know their underwater activity. Although the 146 species of ducks, geese, and swans superficially resemble each other and some may compete, few if any have precisely the same requirements. Each is able to exploit its own special niche in the water world a little more efficiently than the others.

We are reminded all the time that both the birds and their environments evolved together. A hunter who brings down a duck sometimes notices tiny oval leaflets adhering to the feathers. This is duckweed, *Lemna*, which produces few seeds; its principal way of reproducing is to bud. A lobe appears on the small green leaflet which grows and then separates as a daughter plant, capable of reproducing on its own. All marsh ducks eat *Lemna*, which often sticks to them as they swim through masses of it and is thus carried to new ponds and puddles, insuring survival for both ducks and duckweed.

A SPARROW HAWK'S DIET

Because of their high metabolic rate, birds have enormous appetites in proportion to their size and weight: the smaller and lighter the bird, the more prodigious is its food intake. The three piles shown here represent a year's food of a sparrow hawk that breeds and winters in Michigan. The smallest pile, 5 per cent, is insects; the next, 15 per cent, is small birds; the largest, 80 per cent, is rodents. Estimates indicate that a typical sparrow hawk may eat 290 mice in a single year.

Birds of prey, some 400 species strong, divide all nature into parts: day and night. Two thirds of their number—the hawks, eagles, falcons and vultures—are diurnal, going about their business between sunrise and sunset. The other third, the owls, are mainly night hunters. In North America the great horned owl emerges at dusk to prowl over the same terrain where the red-tailed hawk soared at noon. Similarly, the barred owl dominates the swampy woodlands while the red-shouldered hawk sleeps. Nocturnal habits, therefore, are no insurance for the safety of small mammals, every one of which is a potential meal for some predator. The huge binocular eyes of owls have great light-gathering power and their ears, long asymmetrical slits hidden behind the facial disks, can pinpoint the rustling of a mouse in the darkest wood. L. R. Dice, experimenting with long-eared and barn owls, found that they could locate a dead mouse in light ten to one hundred times dimmer than that needed by the human eye, and could capture a live mouse in total darkness.

The method of killing used by a hawk or an owl is to plunge at its prey and to strike or clutch with hooked talons. Vultures usually (but not always) eschew living prey and therefore have no need for the strongly curved "meat hooks" of their diurnal relatives; their feet are relatively weak.

No bird in the world is better equipped for pursuit than the peregrine falcon, bulletheaded, broad in the shoulder and tapering to the tail, a powerful, perfectly streamlined machine whose pointed wings are capable of putting it into a power dive estimated to reach 175 miles per hour. But the peregrine is effective only in open terrain; for this reason falconry as a sport has never caught on in wooded eastern North America as it has on the moorlands of north England and Scotland. Most falcons are strong fliers of the open country, although some of the smaller ones, the kestrels, are more like helicopters, hovering for mice, grasshoppers and other petty prey.

The bird hawks, the *accipiters*, on the other hand, are built for the hedge-hopping technique, the surprise attack. They have evolved a short rounded wing, designed for dodging through the trees and for quick maneuvering. The big goshawk specializes in grouse and small mammals, while the little sharp-shin takes warblers. For every successful try at a bird there are a number of misses. The bird caught, more often than not, is the marginal individual, sick, old or unwary. European sparrow hawks (the equivalent of the American sharp-shin) have become very rare in England during the last decade because, it is believed, they were feeding mainly on songbirds stricken with toxic pesticides, and thus many were fatally stricken themselves.

Contrary to the views held by many sportsmen, the birds of prey are not creatures of pure destruction. Because their victims for the most part are the weak and the unfit, they tone up the vitality of their prey through natural selection—they are necessary to the health of the wildlife community. In the early '50s when the rabbit plague myxomatosis was deliberately introduced into France nearly all the rabbits of western Europe succumbed in blind agony. Mortalities ran between 95 and 99 per cent, but in the Marismas of southern Spain the disease never reached epidemic proportions. There the population of kites, eagles and other birds of prey, more numerous than elsewhere in Europe, caught the infected rabbits so quickly that the disease never succeeded in getting out of hand.

Though large birds of prey like eagles may be forced to live in solitary splendor so that they can maintain a dependable prey population, sociability has its rewards for some species. Vultures are dependent on the accident of death, whether caused by disease, starvation, fire or by that archpredator, man. A windfall often means food for all. Every big-game hunter who has gone on safari in Africa knows how quickly vultures seem to communicate knowledge of a kill. The first soaring birds to spot carrion seem to betray it to more distant birds by their maneuvers. Within the space of minutes a great wheel of birds zeros in on the target while new recruits arrive from all points of the compass. Less than a century ago a hunter who had been killing antelope recorded that no less than 150 California condors were attracted to the scene (there are probably only about 40 of these big birds alive today).

Black vultures were once accused of spreading hog cholera, but actually no more efficient sanitary squad exists than these or, for that matter, vultures in general. Their digestive system destroys bacteria and even their excretions probably are an effective antiseptic, for instead of squirting clear as an eagle does they whitewash their own legs. The head, which comes into contact with putrid flesh, is naked, exposing infectious bacteria to the purifying rays of the sun. The marabou, an African stork with the habits of a vulture, also has a bare head and defecates on its own feet.

The diurnal birds of prey, ranging from six-inch-long pygmy falconets of Asia to the great monkey-eating eagle of the Philippines, have exploited nearly every source of vertebrate prey smaller than themselves. The secretary bird, so-called because it has a score of penlike quills dangling from behind its ears, specializes in snakes and its long legs are protected with heavy plating. The honey buzzard, fond of wasps, actually has protective facial armor, small hard scalelike feathers between the eye and the bill and forehead. The Everglade kite, which feeds only on *Pomacea* snails, carries an exaggerated hook on its upper mandible. For many years ornithologists thought this was for scooping out the snail, but apparently it is not. Instead, the bird patiently holds the mollusk in its talons until it cautiously ventures from its shell; then, with a precise prick, the hook pierces the nerve center and the paralyzed snail is consumed.

Every now and then a bird seems to hit on a special way of making a living. Eons ago a vulture, somewhere in Africa, must have idly pecked at the fruit of an oil palm and, finding it edible, made a habit of feeding on it. Today the palm-nut vulture eats little else except for an occasional dead fish.

In northern South America another aberrant bird specializes in the oily fruits of palms—the unbelievable oilbird, or guacharo. Related to the whippoorwills and nightjars and the only vegetarian among a strictly insectivorous order of birds, it plucks the fruit while hovering like a helicopter. It is said to travel at night as much as 50 miles to find ripe fruit, returning before dawn like one of the tortured demons or lost souls of Bald Mountain to hide in caves so deep and dark that it must employ a sort of sonar to find its way about. Bats have a similar device located in their ears with which they measure the distance of objects by emitting supersonic squeaks. The oilbird's clicks, however, are audible to human ears, with a frequency of about 7,000 cycles per second.

Another group of specialists, the honey guides, give us pause to ponder the intricacies of evolution. Dull-colored and as unprepossessing as sparrows, the greatest claim to oddity of this mainly African family is its addiction to beeswax. One species, the greater honey guide, attracts the attention of a honey badger or a baboon, or even a primitive African tribesman, by chattering and, making sure it is followed, guides him to the bees' nest. Waiting patiently while its partner has a go at the honey, it finally helps itself to the bits of honeycomb lying about. Normally beeswax is indigestible, but Herbert Friedmann recently proved that the bacterial flora within the bird's intestines turn it into useful food.

SOME birds are not averse to poaching and piracy. The bald eagle often highjacks the osprey returning to its eyrie with a fish. The eagle, faster and more powerful, harries the osprey until it drops its catch and, plunging quickly, snatches the fish before it hits the water. Frigate birds harass boobies when they return from their fishing at sea, forcing them to disgorge. Similarly, one whole family of birds, the jaegers and skuas, gull-like sea birds of piratical habits, make their living by raiding gulls and terns.

The widgeon, a dabbling duck, cannot dive easily as does the canvasback. It overcomes this handicap by waiting until the canvasback surfaces with a mouthful of wild celery, then rushes in to snatch it away. Laughing gulls use a similar technique when a brown pelican surfaces with a pouchful of small fish: during the brief moment when the pelican allows the water to drain from its open pouch the gulls snatch their share.

In contrast to the specialists, some birds are true omnivores and will eat almost anything. Crows and jays, always resourceful, will eat young birds in season, as well as baby mice, insects, grain, fruits, or carrion. But even they have their preferences and these may change seasonally.

The question is, what is a balanced diet for a bird? The birds are obviously opportunists, taking whatever is in most plentiful supply within the limits of their various basic needs. Availability is a key factor in all predation, whether it involves the goshawk that takes a pheasant instead of a grouse, or the American robin that eats a tomato worm instead of a Cecropia larva. Probably no bird has ever eliminated its food supply; were it to do so it would eliminate itself. Usually when one item of food becomes scarcer the bird turns to something else within its food spectrum. It crops the expendable surpluses, seldom digging deep into capital. And through the wisdom of natural selection the future takes care of itself.

A NORTHERN SHRIKE STORES ITS FOOD BY IMPALING IT ON TWIGS OR THORNS. HERE THE VICTIMS ARE A GRASSHOPPER AND A SMALL FROG

Food from Every Habitat

One reason birds are so abundant is that they can eat almost anything, not only plants, insects and even mammals of some size but also food that is inaccessible to other creatures. Many are omnivorous and show little specialization. Others, however, which have concentrated on a particular food source, have evolved unique equipment and strange ways for getting—and even storing—a meal.

FLIPPED ON ITS BACK, a brown pelican makes an awkward entry. Although expert divers, they can be upset by sudden gusts or updrafts.

The Master Divers

Some special problems confront air-breathing birds that enter the water to feed on fish and other marine creatures. Whether they plunge from the sky or dive from the surface, they must be able to come up quickly before their air runs out and seize and hold their prey without gulping too much water.

Pelicans, gannets and boobies are among the birds that have solved the resurfacing problem by evolving inflatable air sacs under the skin. These not only make them more buoyant, but also absorb much of the shock of impact. The loon, a surface diver, has learned simply to hold its breath. Although it usually surfaces in less than a minute, it is known to stay under water for as long as five minutes while swimming for hundreds of yards. The osprey, like any hawk, avoids both of these problems by grabbing its victim from the water with razor-sharp talons.

A DIVE-BOMBING ATTACK by brown pelicans begins when the pair peels off, extending their necks and pointing their beaks like spears (left).

ON TARGET, a pelican's dive ends successfully (right). The fish will end up in the pouch along with quarts of water which must be drained.

A GREAT SPOTTED WOODPECKER, faced with the problem of getting a round, rolling hazelnut to stay still long enough to be opened, solves it by ramming the nut into a makeshift vise it has chiseled out of the tree bark, then splits it with a few raps of its beak. For catching insects, this European bird has another weapon—a tongue with tiny barbs at the tip for spearing its prey.

Drills, Hammers, Spoons and Spears

Food that is hard to get at—the kernel in a nut, the grub under the bark of a tree—is the particular specialty of some orders of birds which have evolved highly developed tools designed to perform one job well. Beaks are the primary instruments, and in jays, parrots, nutcrackers and woodpeckers they are as hard as flint, built to gouge, crack, hammer and drill. The common grackle, going still further, has a kind of built-in lathe, a tough ridge in its palate which, as it rotates an acorn in its mouth, literally saws it open. Many woodpeckers, in addition, have long sticky tongues for snapping up insects. The green woodpecker, for example, can send its prying tongue deep into ant tunnels to lap up food (below).

A GREEN WOODPECKER extends its long and sinuous tongue some four inches into the galleries of an ant nest, here cut away and walled off with a pane of glass. The tongue is thickly coated with saliva and flexible enough to follow every curve of the gallery, picking up adults and pupae alike which the bird skillfully works backward toward its bill until it has a mouthful.

A GREEN BARBET of India, its mouth full of berries, drops from its perch an instant before spreading its wings. Although related to the woodpecker, the barbet has a less specialized beak. Instead of chiseling hardwood, it plucks berries or digs for grubs in soft ground or rotted trees. It is a wasteful feeder, harvesting more than it consumes, but does not store its food.

FALLING SILENTLY, a great horned owl aims for the head of an eastern coachwhip snake. Although owls have excellent night vision, they rely on extraordinarily acute hearing for attacks.

The Master Hunters

In a sense, any bird that feeds on another living creature, even an insect, is a predator. But the true birds of prey are those specially equipped to take on larger animals, from mice and rabbits to snakes and small deer—the hawks and eagles which hunt by day, and the owls which take over at night. Ranging in

RUFFLED AND BADLY WINDED, BUT TRIUMPHANT, THE OWL HAS MANAGE

MISJUDGING ITS STRIKE, the owl hits too far back of the snake's head to immobilize it and is knocked flat by its flailing tail. The frantic snake tries to get away but the owl hangs on.

A FURIOUS BATTLE ensues as the owl tries to kill the snake before the latter can coil around the owl's body in an attempt to suffocate it. Such fights can end in death for both combatants.

size from the tiny pygmy falcons of Asia to the great, monkey-eating eagles of the Philippines, the predators rely on sharp-clawed feet, the actual killing instruments, and beaks designed for chopping and ripping. Feet vary according to their use. Thus African hawk eagles have long toes for catching birds on the wing, while owls have short, powerful feet for clutching small mammals and reptiles. All birds of prey have compact, hooked beaks, and the falcon's is notched as well for snapping the neck vertebrae of its victims. Sometimes, as in the case of the owl seen here, a first strike fails and a real fight follows.

TO KEEP ITS GRIP ON THE SNAKE'S BODY WITH BOTH TALONS AND FINISHES IT OFF WITH A LETHAL BITE JUST BACK OF THE VULNERABLE HEAD

SIGHTING A POSSUM, a young red-tailed hawk hunches forward ready to plunge. Red-tails perch for hours at a time on a favorite roost, searching for movements that could mean a meal.

An Apprentice Predator

The business of hunting, while motivated by instinct, is also a craft. Young birds learn it only after long practice, and experience teaches them what they can safely handle in the way of prey. Most immature birds attack whatever tempts them on a hit-or-miss basis until they have had some possibly painful lessons; what they will get will be the very small, the very young, and the very old.

The red-tailed hawk here is an immature bird whose judgment may have been further impaired by

SURPRISED BY THE POSSUM'S SHARP TEETH AND WILLINGNESS TO FIGHT BACK, THE YOUNG RED-TAIL NERVOUSLY FLAPS ITS WINGS AND LURCHES

several weeks spent in captivity. Nevertheless, it belongs to a species that does kill possums, and when this one saw a possum, instinct launched it to the attack. But where an experienced adult bird would have struck fast and hard, the youngster, not quite sure of itself, failed to press its dive all the way home. As a result, instead of having a dead or stunned animal in its talons, it found itself facing one that was very much alive. Thus threatened, it abandoned the attack completely and hurriedly backed away.

CHECKING ITS DIVE too soon, the hawk spreads its wings, apparently sensing the possum may be a bit too big for it. This gives the possum time to scramble around and face its attacker.

BACKWARD. HAND-REARED, THIS BIRD PAID NO ATTENTION TO THE CAMERA BUT BEHAVED AS A WILD HAWK WOULD HAVE IN A SIMILAR SITUATION

The Profits of Fraternization

Like many animals, birds occasionally find their food in association with other creatures, frequently to the benefit of both. The partnership may be one-sided, as in the case of a sparrow picking up seeds from the droppings of other animals, or the ptarmigan, which eats insects dug up by caribou. But sometimes the arrangement is mutually beneficial, as in the cleaning arrangement in which the African tick bird removes vermin from large mammals.

In an extreme example, the honey guide, a small forest bird, will lure a badger to a wild bees' nest by chattering, flying ahead a few feet and chattering again. The badger will find the nest, eat the honey and leave the comb and grubs for the bird. But the red-billed oxpecker (*bottom right*) plays a dual role: it not only acts as a doctor to the rhinoceros, picking ticks from its hide, but it also warns its host of danger with its agitated chatter.

A GRAZING OSTRICH rooting about in search of grass, seeds and insects works over the same African plains territory as a gazelle and a wart hog. Each animal may involuntarily lead the others to a source of food and even alert them to danger.

SCAVENGING GULLS wait for a pair of big Alaskan brown bears to finish their meal of salmon. When the bears depart, the gulls devour whatever is left, an arrangement apparently satisfactory to both parties.

A NIBBLING OXPECKER pulling parasites from a rhinoceros wound secures a meal and helps keep the large animal free of infection. The crowned lapwing in the foreground feeds on insects the rhino turns up.

FLITTING CATTLE EGRETS skip under foot or perch on the backs of African Ankole cattle. Though they feed primarily on the insects stirred up as the cattle graze, they have also found a source of food in the flies on the backs of the cattle themselves.

RUFOUS HORNBILL

ARIEL TOUCAN

PARAKEET

SHOEBILL

KING VULTURE

CARACARA

Beaks Both Useful and Bizarre

The oddly shaped beaks on these pages all have one thing in common: they perform specific functions. Most were shaped by eating habits, though some hornbill species use their great and gaudy bills as a defense against marauding monkeys and snakes, while the toucan's lobster-claw beak serves as a mark of recognition and may figure in courtship display. The carrion-eating king vulture and the caracara have sharp hooks at the tips of their beaks for tearing hides and meat. The shoebill's beak also ends in a hook, but it is flat and serrated as an aid in holding slippery frogs. The parakeet's strong, curved bill is well adapted for cracking seeds, gouging out chunks of fruit, and even for climbing. The protruding lower half of the black skimmer's trowel-like beak is useful for scooping up fish out of water.

A BLACK SKIMMER PICKS UP SMALL FISH ON THE WING BY PLOWING THE WATER WITH ITS LOWER BILL

CANADA GEESE float on a pond in North Carolina after an October flight from their Hudson Bay nesting grounds. With food available at this private refuge, they will remain until the first full moon in March.

4

How Many Birds?

ANY attempt to reduce to manageable proportions a concept as enormous and wide-ranging as the world's population of birds must begin by fitting them into some system of categories. An obvious way to do this is to consider them in terms of their distribution and for more than a century naturalists have been trying out various ways of doing just that. P. L. Sclater was the first to look at the bird population from a worldwide point of view, in 1857, when he suggested a system organized on basic geographical areas, believing like so many other men of his time that every species of animal must have been created within and over the geographic area it occupied.

Sclater's system divided the world into six major regions: the Nearctic, comprising North America north of central Mexico; the Neotropical, including Central and South America; the Palearctic, which took in Europe, the northwest corner of Africa, and Asia without the subcontinent of India and the southeastern peninsular countries; the Ethiopian, including most of Africa and also southern Arabia; the Oriental, comprising tropical India, Burma, Malaysia and the southeast; and the Australian, made up of Australia, New Zealand and the adjacent islands. On a map of the world, this division would appear as six great geographic regions, overlapping here and there as to continents but nonetheless quite clearly delimited and defined. Darwin's theories in the *Origin of Species*, published soon after, knocked the props from under Sclater's basic reasoning about the geographic origin of animals, but his concept of zoogeographical regions, for reasons of practicality is still accepted with some modifications by naturalists today. For example, because of the massive intermingling of New World and Old World birds in the more northern areas where they have crossed the Bering Strait between Asia and America, many biologists prefer to lump the Nearctic and Palearctic into one major region called the Holarctic.

A NORTH AMERICAN concept was worked out some 35 years after Sclater's worldwide system by Clinton Hart Merriam after climbing one of the San Francisco Peaks in Arizona. Starting in the desert, Merriam noted that as he ascended higher and higher the bird life of the areas he passed through changed. As he left the desert area many species dropped behind, to be replaced by others among the piñon pines and still others as he reached the higher fir forests. The birds and other animals were obviously associated with the plant life, and climbing the mountain was like traveling northward, with altitude compensating for latitude. Though other naturalists had noticed this before him, Merriam was the first to see it as a practical demonstration of a method by which the distribution of North American plants and animals could be described. His mountain was, in effect, a map set up on end, with various "life zones" succeeding each other from the desert upward, like broad belts circling the mountain.

From this concept, Merriam developed a new system for categorizing plants and animals, based not on geographical areas but on regions of characteristic temperature and humidity. These two, he wrote, "are the most important causes governing distribution and . . . temperature is more potent than humidity." He divided the mountain and its environs into seven zones: the Alpine at the summit; the sub-Alpine at the timberline; the Hudsonian in the area of the spruce forests; the Canadian in the area of the Douglas fir; the Neutral Zone, where the ponderosa pines began; the Piñon Pine Zone; and finally, the Desert Zone. Since the first four zones had certain northern influences in common, he lumped them into a major category, the Boreal Division. The last two zones being definitely southern he put together in the Sonoran Division, and the Neutral Zone was later to become known as the Transition Zone, where northern influences blended into southern.

Merriam's concept of "life zones" was subsequently extended to include all of North America. Spread out on a map, they would look like a series of broad, irregular belts marked by lines of equal temperature running principally east and west in their broad outlines but with large areas appearing as islands or peninsulas where one zone, higher or lower than the surrounding territory, intrudes upon another. For more than a generation every regional bird book published in the U.S. followed Merriam's terminology in describing the ranges of birds. Thus we learned that the black-throated green warbler breeds chiefly in the Canadian and Transition Zones, relatively northern or high regions of conifers, while the cactus wren breeds mainly in the Lower Sonoran Zone.

During the last two decades Merriam's system has fallen into disuse because the botanists pointed out that he based too much on temperature and that his use of isothermal lines running from east to west was often illogical. Instead, they devised the biome concept based on the major landscape units, such as grasslands, deciduous forest, coniferous forest, tundra, desert and so on, with a broad blend zone, or ecotone, between each major area. Following this system, the aspen groves of the western foothills, for instance, become the ecotone between the grassland biome and the coniferous forest biome.

Within the biomes there are smaller areas, or developmental stages, which, in time, if left alone will again assume the major characteristics of the biome. For example, if a conifer forest is burned, it grows back at first into bracken and low brush, then into aspen and birch and finally into conifers again. The aspen and birch, however, although they are deciduous trees, are not part of the deciduous biome, but rather a developmental stage of the coniferous biome.

All of these concepts have their logic and their applicability to plant and animal life, but none of them entirely satisfies the ornithologist's desire to fit birds into a coherent distribution pattern. In the burned conifer forest mentioned above, redstarts and red-eyed vireos will nest for a while in the aspen and birch, but that does not mean that they belong to that biome or even to that one life zone. The thing that is important to them is second growth deciduous trees; whether they be aspen and birch or not, that is where they find their niche.

THE horned lark shows a similar disregard of zones. In North America it is to be found in summer from the dry Mexican tablelands to the arctic tundra, while in the Old World it nests spottily from the North African deserts to the edge of the arctic sea. Considered merely geographically, or even from the biome or life zone concepts, this is a confusing distribution indeed—but the important thing to a horned lark is broad expanses of short grass, be they desert grasslands, plains or tundra. In Audubon's day breeding larks had not yet invaded the wooded northeast, but today they nest from Virginia to New England, where their favorite habitats are golf courses and airports—man-made "prairies."

There are cases, however, where birds of the same species occupy totally different environments in various parts of their ranges. The common raven, one of the most widely distributed birds in the Northern Hemisphere, lives in such dissimilar terrain as the waterless Sahara, the coniferous forests of Canada and Siberia, the sea cliffs of western North America and Scandinavia, and the tundra

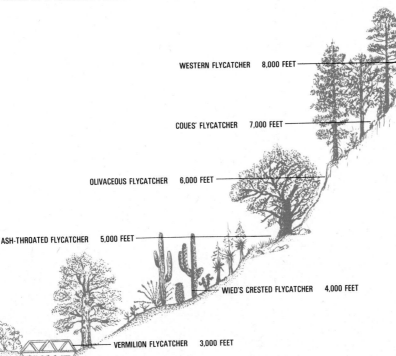

WESTERN FLYCATCHER   8,000 FEET

COUES' FLYCATCHER   7,000 FEET

OLIVACEOUS FLYCATCHER   6,000 FEET

ASH-THROATED FLYCATCHER   5,000 FEET

WIED'S CRESTED FLYCATCHER   4,000 FEET

VERMILION FLYCATCHER   3,000 FEET

SPECIFIC SPOTS FOR SPECIFIC BIRDS

Bird distribution is closely tied to food. This is most clearly shown on a mountainside where different bird species tend to sort themselves into zones matching the bands of vegetation. On a typical mountain in southern Arizona (left), several species of flycatchers may be found. On the plain at its base, the vermilion flycatcher flits among streamside cottonwood trees, and is followed by the Wied's crested flycatcher on the low slopes, where giant cactus replaces the trees. Going up the slope, a new species is dominant about every thousand feet, ending with the western flycatcher among the fir and aspen near the top.

81

and the islands of the arctic sea. The common denominator, if there is one at all, seems to be wilderness.

The fact is that although some birds can be made to fit the life zone concept or the biome concept, both systems are an oversimplification that tends to ignore the evidence of evolutionary processes. Nature is dynamic, defying neat pigeon-holing. Each species, to survive, must be able to exploit a niche just a bit different from that of its neighbors. If the ranges of all 8,580 bird species were plotted on one great world map, their boundaries would seldom coincide, except on some islands, nor would their habitats be precisely the same. The resulting map would be as diffuse as a rainbow.

WHAT is the world population of birds? James Fisher, the British ornithologist, has estimated that the number is in the order of 100 billion. My own estimate for the United States, made some years ago, was that there are not less than five billion breeding land birds and probably closer to six billion at the beginning of summer, or two and a half to three birds per acre. This was based on the breeding-bird censuses of the National Audubon Society, which use singing males on territory as an index to the number of pairs per acre in different types of terrain. Another estimate by Leonard Wing, using a more complicated formula than my rather rough mathematics, came up with a summer population of about 5.6 billion. Neither of these estimates, which might better be called guesstimates, has been challenged during the 20 years since we made them, although I now think they may be a bit high. Both estimates were for the United States south of the Canadian border and did not include Canada and Alaska, a combined area more than 140 per cent as large, where during the summer months an equally large population must be resident. Add to this an average of two young birds successfully fledged for each pair and we have a late summer figure for North America north of Mexico that may be as high as 20 billion. In the light of this, Fisher's estimate of 100 billion for the several continents seems reasonable.

Just how many hundreds of millions or billions of sea birds roam the seven seas is anyone's guess, but although they comprise only three per cent of the

A GROWING FOREST AND ITS CHANGING BIRDS

It is the same rock in all five of these pictures, but they span more than 50 years—the time it may take an open meadow to return to mature forest. At each stage of its development the landscape attracts different birds. In the first scene, a meadowlark has found the abundance of grass and open space that it needs. In the second, the meadowlark has departed; short, woody plants have taken root and a song sparrow has moved in. In the third, more bushes and saplings appear and with them the brush-loving indigo bunting, replacing the song sparrow. In scene four a young, or second-growth, forest has become established along with birds like the redstart, which gleans insects from the leaves. In the last picture the forest is mature and some of the trees are dying, prey to woodboring insects that attract woodpeckers.

MEADOWLARK

SONG SPARROW

world's bird species they probably make up more than three per cent of the total population. Their way of life is a demanding one, but they have few predators and they live for a long time. The period of basic training itself is relatively long. Unlike land birds, which may breed at the age of a year, most sea birds must wait several years before they are sufficiently adept at navigating the sea and wresting a living from it to be able to feed mouths other than their own. A royal albatross may be nine years out of the parental nest before it again touches land and reproduces for the first time. It takes this long to master the art of being an albatross, which as Fisher comments, is probably the most exacting occupation in the bird world. And not only do many sea birds delay their first nesting for a considerable period, but when they do breed they lay relatively small clutches of eggs. Albatrosses, petrels, shearwaters, sooty terns, tropicbirds, most auks and many of the other truly pelagic birds lay only one egg, but this single egg is enough to maintain their population level.

In fact, some of the world's most abundant birds are oceanic. Darwin once wrote that he believed the fulmar (a gull-like petrel) to be the commonest bird in the world. Fisher, the world authority on the fulmar, disagrees: although there may be several millions of fulmars, he states, there are certainly not hundreds of millions. He suggests that the most abundant sea bird may well be Wilson's petrel, a swallow-sized storm petrel that makes the journey to the north Atlantic every summer from its breeding grounds at the edge of the antarctic. Also enormously abundant are many of the shearwaters, which look like small, tube-nosed gulls. A single flock of slender-billed shearwaters off Bass Strait, Australia, was once computed to number more than 150 million birds.

Penguin colonies often number into the hundreds of thousands and an aggregation of five million Adélie penguins has been recorded in a single group of islands. Sooty tern colonies on islands in the Indian Ocean have been reported to exceed a million birds and many colonies of auks in arctic and subarctic waters surpass that figure. No one knows how many dovekies or little auks live on the inaccessible cliffs of Greenland, Iceland and Spitsbergen. Certainly millions, and the Atlantic puffin, a relative of the little auk, has been estimated to

INDIGO BUNTING

REDSTART

HAIRY WOODPECKER

number roughly 15 million. Undoubtedly the largest, single bird city in North America, with perhaps several million birds of a dozen species, is on the great cliffs of Staraya Artil on the island of St. George in the Pribilofs. But even this aggregation is outnumbered by the guano birds—perhaps more than 10 million strong—on the islands off the desert coast of Peru.

Finland is one of the very few countries with a fairly accurate estimate of its total bird population. The Finnish ornithologist Einari Merikalio has boldly attempted to evaluate his country's avifauna by using a technique called the line strip method. Each year during June and early July for 15 years, from 1941 to 1956, he made daily transects of the countryside, following a track which formed an enclosed square exactly one kilometer on each side. Each bird seen or heard was duly noted. His researches carried him into every corner of the country, from the Gulf of Finland to the arctic, and indicated not only that there were approximately 64 million birds in Finland, or about 1.3 birds per acre, but the approximate number of each species.

IN Great Britain one gets the impression of many birds because of the relative abundance of the birds of garden and roadside. Actually, the total number of breeding land birds in England, Scotland and Wales has been estimated to be in the neighborhood of 120 million—slightly over two birds per acre. This figure was arrived at by counting the birds in sample acreages of different environments, using the singing male method. Although gardens and estates in England often average 30 birds per acre, extensive grass country and moorland, with less than one bird per acre, pull the average down.

In the United States the greatest density of land birds is undoubtedly in the colonies of the tricolored blackbird in California, a bird very much like the familiar red-winged blackbird, except that it is highly colonial. Tricolored blackbird colonies may harbor as many as 200,000 pairs and may average between 5,000 and 10,000 nests per acre.

If we are to rule out colonial birds, densities of nesting land birds in the United States, as documented by the Audubon Breeding Bird Census, run from less than one bird per acre on prairies and short-grass plains to 15 or 16 in some rich bogs, swamp-bordered islands and southern hardwood forests. It is quite likely that some marshes support even higher densities, as do suburban estates where the birds have been built up by artificial feeding, nest boxes and berry-bearing shrubs. The average healthy woodland harbors four or five nesting birds per acre, but a wood that has been stripped of its undergrowth by browsing animals may support less than one bird per acre.

About 50 years ago, Wells Cook of the U.S. Department of Agriculture made an extensive survey of the bird populations in rural country. His findings, made known in 1915, showed that U.S. farms averaged about two birds per acre. If we are to assume that there are about 1,124,000,000 acres of farmland in the United States, including croplands, pasturelands, and farm wood lots, the birds would number about 2.25 billion, more than one third the total bird population in the country. However, since 1915, when Cook published his report, the use of pesticides, many of them lethal to bird life, has increased enormously, and over large sections of farmland countless birds have succumbed. In a single year one billion pounds of chemical pesticides may be sprayed over approximately 100 million of the 358 million acres of cropland under cultivation. Censuses taken in cultivated fields in recent years reveal extremely low populations, ranging from zero to a meager eight or nine pairs on 100 acres. It is not improbable that since

World War II our continental bird population has been reduced by many millions, by DDT and its more potent derivatives.

The tropics, rich in variety, seem to support more birds acre by acre than northern regions. Few tropical censuses have been taken except in Mexico, but it is my impression that in some of the scrub-covered grasslands in East Africa, particularly in southern Kenya, densities might well exceed 40 birds per acre.

Not every acre of land is blessed with nesting birds; we have been speaking of averages. Away from the polar icecaps, perhaps the largest areas of birdless country are such lifeless stretches as the Atacama Desert in Chile, lying between the coast and the high Andes, a 600-mile-long wasteland as sterile as an operating table. In the United States the Bonneville salt flats west of Great Salt Lake in Utah are certainly the largest birdless area.

Where would the world's highest density be? In the flamingo concentrations of the Rift Valley in Kenya and Tanganyika it is not exceptional to have more than a million lesser flamingos in one tight-packed, milling mass. But terns, cormorants and auks take up less space than flamingos. At Isla Raza in the Gulf of California 40,000 elegant terns may nest on a single acre; many eggs are but nine inches apart. Among land birds, the swarming colonies of queleas, or locust birds, in Africa defy description. These tiny weaver finches, which may gather in flocks of a million or more, recall tales of the passenger pigeons: they are so numerous that they darken the sky and break large limbs of trees when they settle. Farmers regard them as an agricultural menace and fight them with flame throwers and explosives.

What is North America's number one bird? Is it the house sparrow, introduced from England? Almost certainly not; the starling, less restricted to cities and farms, now outnumbers it. The American robin, however, is a more likely candidate than either. Found from coast to coast, it inhabits cities and forests alike and is one of the most abundant birds in the vast, 3,000-mile belt of conifers stretching across Canada to Alaska. Recently it has been suggested that the red-winged blackbird may be the most numerous bird south of the Canadian border. Nesting not only in every state but probably in every county, it seems to be having a population explosion. Winter roosts often number in the millions.

WHAT are the rarest North American birds? Two are so close to the void of extinction that their existence has been questioned in recent years. The Eskimo curlew, a shore bird with a slender curved bill, was once abundant on the American plains during its passage from the Argentine to the arctic. Killed off for sport and for food before shore birds were removed from the game list, it went unrecorded for a number of years. However, in April 1959, a single bird appeared at Galveston Island on the coast of Texas and one was seen there the following two springs. In 1962 there were two; one was photographed.

The unadaptable ivory-billed woodpecker, North America's largest woodpecker, has not been recorded with certainty for some 10 years, but reports of it still persist and it is just possible that some are valid. The Everglade kite, a snail-eating hawk of the Okeechobee region of Florida, has numbered less than a dozen individuals in some years, the last of the species in the United States. From southern Mexico to Argentina, however, it is still found; it is even possible to see a hundred in a day's drive south of Buenos Aires.

There are now some 50 whooping cranes in the world, seven of them in captivity. Each autumn the eyes of two nations, Canada and the U.S., are on the small surviving company of wild whoopers as they make the hazardous journey between the only known nesting area in Wood Buffalo Park in north Alberta to their wintering ground on the Texas coast. In 1941, its blackest year, this species was at an all-time low of 17; it almost trebled its numbers in the next 25 years, but its survival is still in doubt.

Next on the list is the California condor, the North American bird with the greatest wing span. Living in the rugged coast range north and west of Los Angeles, its numbers have dropped from 60 to 40 in recent decades.

There are probably not more than 50 species of birds whose world populations are known. Rare birds that are conspicuous, such as cranes and condors, can sometimes be counted beak by beak. Sea birds restricted to single colonies on islands can also be assessed. Latest reports from the Galápagos Islands, for example, state that there are at least 2,000 pairs of Galápagos albatrosses on Hood Island, exclusive of those at sea; about 500 flightless cormorants on Albemarle and Narborough, and perhaps a similar number of Galápagos penguins.

Game birds and species of economic importance are often intensively surveyed. When the U.S. Fish and Wildlife Service was put under pressure to open a season on the sandhill crane a preliminary census showed a population of about 100,000, most of which nest in the arctic.

THE only songbird whose continental population is accurately known is Kirtland's warbler. This gray-backed, yellow-breasted bird, restricted to jack pines in several counties in Michigan, was counted almost to the last bird by Harold Mayfield and his associates, who are confident that the number is very close to 1,000. But going from such local ranges to continental distribution is difficult. While we know that there are about 10 million chaffinches in Great Britain and 10.6 million in Finland, these birds are also found from North Africa to central Asia, and it would take an army of census takers to sample their whole range. A rash guess at the chaffinch's world population? More than 200 million.

Territory, the area defended by individual birds, is an important concept in understanding bird populations. Home owners often report robins, cardinals or other birds buffeting against their windows. These misguided creatures apparently mistake their reflections in the glass for other birds of their kind and are bent on driving them away. Each male is a property owner, a status seeker. By holding territory, birds space themselves out, assuring themselves of a stable food supply during the critical nesting period. They do not sing for the joy of singing so much as to proclaim property rights. Song is a challenge to rivals: "This is my land—keep off!"

Birds, then, tend to limit their own numbers. The unemployed birds wander widely and are kept on the move by the more successful males, who see them off with a song and a brisk flurry if necessary. If by some chance a predator catches one of the established males, his place is quickly filled by the next free-lancing prospector. To determine the extent of this replacement, biologists of the U.S. Fish and Wildlife Service in a drastic but useful experiment attempted to kill all the males in a 40-acre tract of forest in Maine. Other males moved in to take their places and although these too were killed the number that came in the following year was nearly the same as before. Nature, like a bank, keeps a surplus to cover losses. Conversely, shooting hawks or foxes or even cats will not result in more birds, for in the absence of predators other natural checks will act as levelers—catastrophes during migration or bad weather, disease, parasites, starvation, or perhaps most effective of all, the birds themselves, practicing birth control through their tradition of defending territory.

THE EDGE OF EXTINCTION

ESKIMO CURLEW

The Eskimo curlew was hunted with such greed along the whole length of its migratory route, from the Canadian tundra south to Argentina, that by 1925 it was reported extinct. Several individuals have been sighted in Texas, however, since 1959.

IVORY-BILLED WOODPECKER

North America's rarest bird, if indeed it is still extant, the ivory-billed woodpecker may number a few individuals in the southern United States. To survive, it needs large stands of virgin timber—and the primeval forests are virtually gone.

Consider for a moment what would happen without these checks. If a single pair of robins holding down a territory of an acre and a half succeeded in the spring of 1960 in raising its two broods of four young, there would be 10 robins by the end of the season. This could happen. But suppose this pair and their progeny escaped all the problems that robins are heir to, had 100 per cent success with their families and all of their descendants survived year after year. By the end of 10 years (the possible life span of the first pair), in the spring of 1970, there would be 19,531,250 robins instead of two—nearly 300 robins for every square foot of the acre and a half!

Agriculturists often debate whether birds really control insects. Undeniably, poison sprays are temporarily more efficient; birds do not do the complete job. But birds working in concert with predatory insects and parasites keep most insect populations in some sort of equilibrium. However, during epidemic outbreaks of certain insects the birds, though prospering, cannot reduce the eruption to a normal level. In a Canadian forest suffering from an outbreak of spruce budworm, nesting warblers may build up to an extraordinary density. During one such outbreak S. Charles Kendeigh recorded that in one area 88 pairs of bay-breasted warblers alone had territories averaging scarcely more than a third of an acre in extent.

Insect boom is followed by insect bust. Starvation, not predation by the birds, seems to be the main factor that brings things into line again—starvation when the insects have eaten themselves out of house and home. The birds, at peak abundance because of their earlier nesting success, are now hard put to find food. Unless they can find other food somewhere, their numbers, too, may go into a sharp decline.

It is quite likely that more birds have cyclic ups and downs than we recognize. We witness the irregular movements of some of the boreal Canadian birds —crossbills, pine grosbeaks, redpolls, Bohemian waxwings and others. Some winters they visit the northern United States in great flocks, quickening the pulse of the field-glass fraternity; then for several years we do not see them, nor can we predict the next invasion. We cannot seem to fit them into a cyclic pattern; they are irruptive. On the other hand, the northern shrike, a songbird that preys on mice, seems to be tied in with the four-year vole cycle. When these mice crash, which often coincides with the lemming crash, the shrikes leave their open subarctic forest and are to be seen in considerable numbers in the northern United States.

BECAUSE grouse are important game species, sportsmen have long been aware of their fluctuations. In North America the ruffed grouse has a cycle that varies between 9 and 11 years. The red grouse of Britain is more irregular; its cycle may be anywhere from 3 to 10 years between peaks. In Scandinavia, the willow ptarmigan, a grouse that goes white in winter, has a 3-to-4-year cycle.

The famous lemming cycle averages four years, varying between three and five, and when these little arctic rodents build up to a point where they start their suicidal wanderings, the snowy owls, the rough-legged hawks and all the other mouse-eating predators wax fat and raise large broods. But then, at just about the time these birds reach their peak, the lemmings go into a population tailspin. The snowy owls, which in other years stay in the far north, are then forced to wander in search of other food. Many reach the northern United States, particularly along the Atlantic coast, around the Great Lakes and on the northern prairies. During one particularly great flight in the winter

CALIFORNIA CONDOR

For the California condor, the largest of all North American vultures, the change-over from ranches to fruit farms has meant a diminishing supply of the carrion on which it feeds. The surviving 40 birds are protected in their mountain refuge.

NÉNÉ

Although the inroads of man reduced the néné, or Hawaiian goose, population to a low point of 30 in 1951, the birds seem to be making a comeback. Bred in captivity in England, Hawaii and elsewhere, they now have a total population of about 500.

of 1945 and 1946, there were 13,502 reports of these big, white owls filed by ornithologists from southern Canada and the northern United States.

The goshawk, a powerful predator of the Canadian forest, is linked with the 10-year cycle of the varying hare and ruffed grouse. In the years when it is forced to travel south it turns its attentions to cottontails and pheasants.

Although voles are apparently not cyclic in Britain, there is on record a great plague of voles on the Scottish border in 1891 and 1892. Short-eared owls moved in and capitalized on the situation by raising exceptionally large broods of 8 to 10 young. Their abnormally extended breeding season, from February to July, suggests that some had more than one brood. When the voles crashed, the owls moved out, but many were found dead of starvation. A similar situation existed in Scotland in 1952 and 1953.

The ranges of birds are not static. Contrast the limited domains today of the condor, the whooping crane, the swallow-tailed kite and the trumpeter swan with their ranges of a century ago. On the credit side of the ledger, during the last few decades the continued warming of climate in the Northern Hemisphere has favored the northward spread of many species. Recently, birds of central Europe have gained a foothold in Scandinavia and during the last half century no less than nine continental species have established themselves in Iceland. Similarly, on our own continent, cardinals, Carolina wrens, tufted titmice and other "southern" birds are now invading New England.

Occasionally, wind-drifted strays consolidate a beachhead far from home. In January, 1937, a number of fieldfares from Norway were carried on a high wind to Greenland where they manage to survive to this day in the birch groves of fiords near the southern tip. Had they encountered their New World relative, the robin, which does not live in Greenland, it is unlikely that the fieldfares would have withstood the competition. Less fortunate were some 1,000 lapwings that made the crossing from Ireland to Newfoundland in 24 hours during a strong easterly gale in 1927. They all perished because of the winter weather. It is likely that most such wanderers die, although all oceanic islands where land birds exist must have been populated originally by strays.

THE most successful invaders in recent times have usually had some assist by man—the starling, the house sparrow, not to mention some of the transplanted game species. However, no one knows how the cattle egret of Africa made the jump from the Old World to the New. It arrived, undetected at first among the other white herons, in British Guiana, to be first noticed in the late 1930s. In 1952 it appeared on the Atlantic seaboard of the United States. By 1962 the bird was breeding as far north as New Jersey and Ontario, and roosts of as many as 30,000 were reported in Florida. This is certainly the most spectacular bird invasion in our time.

Thus the bird population, locally as well as on a worldwide scale, is in subtle but constant flux. One winter, cardinals may flock around the feeding stations of Connecticut, bringing delight to suburban home owners; the next year a glimpse of one or two of them may be a rarity. An influx of a new and different species may cause bird watchers in one locality to go scrambling for their binoculars and record books, while elsewhere a long stable population will be on the wane. It is just this that makes birds so endlessly fascinating to all who have ever given them more than cursory attention: as great as is the pleasure of recognizing old friends as the seasons change, the constant expectation of meeting new ones is a greater pleasure still.

A FLOCK OF KNOTS, MIGRATING SOUTH FROM THE ARCTIC, RESTS ON THE ENGLISH COAST. THEY MAY FLY AS FAR AS WEST AFRICA

100,000,000,000 Birds

From polar icecaps to humid jungles, the world's billions of birds extract a living from every kind of environment. In the tropics the rich variety of food gives rise to an amazing variety of species. By contrast, the colder regions support only a few species, but these, mostly sea birds which feed on the teeming hordes of fish abounding in icy currents, frequently live in crowded colonies of millions.

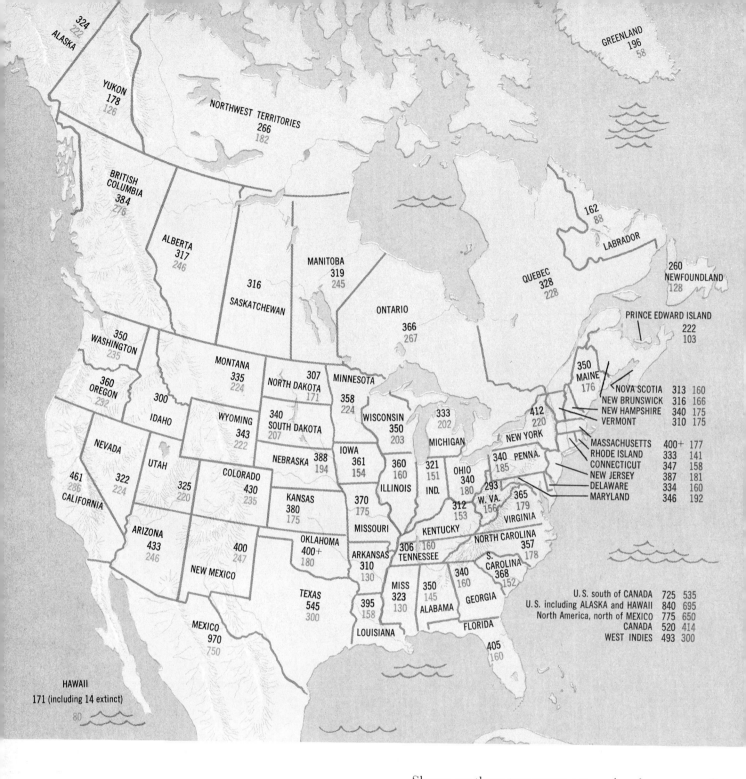

A Census of Species

Shown on these two maps are regional censuses of birds by species in North America and Europe. This up-to-date breakdown by state, province and country is the first published attempt to present such an over-all survey. Its current population figures were obtained from approximately 100 leading ornithologists throughout the world. The black figure in each case represents the total number of species known to have occurred in each area and includes permanent residents, summer and winter visitors, migrants and occasional or accidental visitors. The

ICELAND
231
76

FINLAND
328
203

SWEDEN
356
240

ALL EUROPE (EXCLUSIVE OF U.S.S.R.) 577 420

NORWAY
333
220

U.S.S.R.
704
622

JAPAN   425 218
INDIA   1,125 920
CHINA (including Tibet) 1,100
KOREA   360
OUTER MONGOLIA 300

IRELAND
338
133

440
190

DENMARK 341 183
HOLLAND 364 184
BELGIUM 343 148

GREAT BRITAIN
(England, Scotland,
and Wales)

POLAND
370
230

GERMANY
435
250

CZECHOSLOVAKIA
300
190

AUSTRIA
338
215

HUNGARY
332
185

ROMANIA
345
240

FRANCE
441
260

SWITZ.
347
186

YUGOSLAVIA
236

BULGARIA
338
236

PORT.

ITALY
450
232

339
204

GREECE

315
180

SPAIN
397
225

colored figure represents the number of species
that have been recorded as breeding.

No fossils or subspecies are included in these totals, but they do include foreign species successfully introduced as well as a few species that have
become extinct in recent times.

No record has been included that is not based
on a collected specimen, a recognizable photograph
or a well-documented sight record by at least two
competent observers. In cases where a figure is missing, such as the total number of species that have

been reported in Yugoslavia or the number that
breed in Idaho, it was left out because no figure was
available at this time.

All these totals are approximate. They will inevitably grow as more and more species are recorded by more observers. For areas such as Great
Britain, Massachusetts and New York, the figures
may seem a bit inflated—reflecting the work of ar-
mies of bird watchers who have been studying those
areas for many years. Today their chance of finding new birds, though not remote, is diminishing.

A COLONY OF MURRES NESTS ON TOP OF A ROCKY PINNACLE OFF THE BRITISH COAST AS KITTIWAKE GULLS BREED ON THE LOWER LEDGES

Rigors and Rewards of a Crowded Life

Birds colonize for different reasons. They may be naturally gregarious. They may be gaining protection from predators, conserving body heat in a cold climate, exploiting the neighborhood's food supply, or any combination of these things. A scarcity of nesting places may force birds into a communal life, sometimes even with other species, on the few good sites that are available. This is true of the murres, the weak-winged northern counterparts of the flightless penguins.

Murres colonize for still another reason: to mate and breed successfully, they need to be stimulated by the noisy encouragement of a crowd. Thus, they are found in tightly packed and exuberant masses on the cliffs and pinnacles of islands on rocky northern coasts, thousands nesting together, each almost a pecking distance apart from its neighbors. Those

who start to breed first form the center of the colony, where they are safest from the raids of predators. When a young murre is nearly three weeks out of the egg and its wings are still only half grown, it becomes restless and, with only a little parental urging, jumps off the cliff and begins to fend for itself.

Much of the murres' pattern of life is duplicated by the penguins in the bottom half of the world because both birds have been molded by similar environments and similar problems in making a living. Like the murres, penguins also return to the same breeding ground year after year and they help raise each other's young in nurseries. But there is a maverick colony of penguins too: though most people associate these natty birds with the cold wastes of the antarctic ice, a colony of about 250 individuals lives in the Galápagos Islands, astride the equator.

SPLASHING IN THE SURF, Magellanic penguins scurry away from the photographer who has discovered their colony in the Straits of Magellan. Unlike the murres of northern coasts, which nest only on rocky cliffs and pinnacles, Magellanic penguins will live on almost any kind of coast—scrub, rain forest or grassy moor—as long as it is suitable for digging their burrow nests.

The Biggest Bird Colony

Food is one of the most important single reasons why birds form colonies, and food is the dominating factor in the biggest bird colony on earth. Its inhabitants, some 10 million strong, are the Peruvian boobies and cormorants that live on the hot, arid islands off the coast of Peru. They feast on the billions of anchovies in the cold Humboldt Current flowing just offshore, and the droppings from this rich diet form the finest natural fertilizer in the world—guano.

The guano birds' harvesting of the anchovies is systematic and endless. After small squadrons have searched the sea for schools of fish, the birds attack in force. Thousands at a time hiss into the sea like spears, vanishing in a geyser of foam. Again and again they dive until at last, darkening the sky, they return to their island homes. Their colonies are so crowded, at about three families to the square yard, that government wardens can count the population by simply measuring a colony's dimensions.

The unique value of the guano colonies as fertilizer factories has been recognized for more than 1,000 years, and the birds themselves were placed under strict protection by the Incas. Later, however, they were so severely exploited that in 1909 Peru was forced to set up a guano administration to regulate the harvesting and, once again, protect the birds.

SACKS OF GUANO are stacked in rows by squads of workers on a Peruvian coastal island. By government law, the removals of guano may not exceed the amounts left annually by the birds.

WHITE PLUMAGE GLEAMING, thousands of boobies nest on Peru's South Guañape Island. Building up about six inches of guano a century, birds have created deposits as deep as 150 feet.

A STARTLED SKYFUL of flamingos shatters the stillness of the morning above their native Camargue, a desolate land of brackish swamps and salt flats in the estuaries of the Rhone River.

Long hunted for its plumage, this shy and beautiful bird is now protected in its remote mud cities by the French government. Mating, nest building, incubating the egg, feeding the young—

everything that a flamingo does in its life, it does in large colonies. While it is true that this need for community living is exhibited by birds at all levels, ornithologists have found that it is particularly true of large birds on the lower rungs of the evolutionary ladder, where the instinctive drives seem to be reinforced by the sight of thousands of others acting the same way.

5

The Riddle of Migration

SINCE first he watched the flight of birds, man has pondered their disappearance in the fall and their reappearance in the spring. A familiar passage in the Bible from Jeremiah (VIII, 7) long ago noted the regularity of these seasonal comings and goings: "Yea, the stork in the heaven knoweth her appointed times; and the turtle [dove] and the crane and the swallow observe the time of their coming."

It was a most intriguing mystery and many different answers were offered. Aristotle, the foremost naturalist of antiquity, acknowledged that some birds migrate "as in the case of the crane. . . . Pelicans also migrate and fly from the Strymon to the Ister," but he stated on the other hand that: "A great number of birds also go into hiding; they do not all migrate, as is generally supposed, to warmer countries. . . . The stork, the ouzel, the turtle dove and the lark, all go into hiding." Aristotle also introduced a third possibility—transmutation. He announced unequivocally that the European robin changed at the approach of summer into the European redstart.

For 2,000 years, especially during the uncritical Middle Ages, these ancient pronouncements were repeated by countless authors who elaborated on the writings of their predecessors without examining nature firsthand. An exception was Frederick II, the Holy Roman Emperor, perhaps the only student of migration of his day, who in his monumental book *The Art of Falconry*, written about 1245, included 11 chapters on this subject.

Down through the centuries the ingenuity of people in explaining the seasonal avicycle reached new heights of fancy. Migration was now accepted in the case of many of the big birds, but the tiny birds, naturalists rationalized, got across the oceans by hitching rides on the backs of their larger fellows. Still later, the most bizarre theory of all was published, perhaps tongue in cheek, in 1703 by an Englishman who described himself as "a person of learning and piety." He wrote that birds flew to the moon, taking 60 days to get there and that on arrival, finding no nourishment, they went into hibernation!

It seems inconceivable that Linnaeus, who devised the modern system of zoological nomenclature, should have written in his *Systema Naturae* in 1735 that the house martin "lives under the roof in European houses; it is immersed during the winter but comes out in the spring." Even his famous contemporary, Gilbert White of Selborne, accepted the view that swallows hibernated in the mud, although he did admit: "We must not, I think, deny migration in general; because migration certainly does subsist in some places, as my brother in Andalusia has fully informed me."

THE ghost of bird hibernation had finally been laid to rest—so everybody thought—for a century, when, in December, 1946, Dr. Edmund C. Jaeger and two companions, exploring a canyon in the Chuckawalla Mountains in southeastern California, discovered a poorwill, a small night bird of the whippoorwill type, tucked into a rocky crevice. Suspecting it to be dead, they were surprised when the bird blinked an eye. They kept it under observation for four successive winters and always the same bird was to be found in deathlike lethargy in the crevice. One winter it remained inactive for 88 days. A series of tests showed that its temperature dropped to 64.6° F. (the normal temperature of an active poorwill is about 106° F.). A light beam directed into its eye elicited no response; a mirror held up to its nostrils showed no condensation of moisture; a stethoscope could not detect a heartbeat. Yet, when spring temperatures stirred the bird to life it was seen to fly away. The southwestern Indians apparently knew the secret of the poorwill: the Hopis call it *Hölchko*, "the sleeper."

Torpidity has been observed in captive lesser nighthawks, relatives of the poorwill. Hummingbirds may go into a torpor at night and even on cold days. European swifts have been found in a torpid state in France and white-throated swifts in a similar comatose condition have been recorded in winter on Slover Mountain in California. But whether such birds have the ability to go from torpor into true hibernation remains to be proved.

In a broad sense, migration, derived from the Latin *migrare* (to go from one place to another), means any traveling. The ability to move about is almost universal among animals; they are not rooted to their environment as are the plants. But used in its strict sense the term often implies no return, and the words invasion, dispersal, immigration or emigration are perhaps preferable. When applied to birds, migration usually means a two-way journey, a yearly round trip. Because of the gift of wings an individual bird can exploit two different parts of the world, a flexibility which gives it an advantage denied to more sedentary creatures.

During the brief arctic summer there is vast elbowroom in the tundra for golden plovers and other shore birds, but for eight or nine months of the year no shore bird could survive there. However, the pampas of Argentina, 8,000 miles distant, offer a comparable living. By traveling, the golden plover enjoys two summers each year and knows not a hint of winter. On the other hand, the willow ptarmigan, an arctic grouse that turns white in winter, stays in the frozen north. It shifts its diet from insects to the buds and twigs of willows and alders. The migratory movement of the ptarmigan, if it takes place at all, may simply be dispersal, or it may be a short journey from the bleaker slopes to more protected valleys. The latter kind of movement has been called "altitudinal migration" and many mountain birds practice it. Altitude, as noted in the previous chapter, compensates to some extent for latitude; a journey down a mountain slope to a spot 4,000 feet lower would be the rough equivalent of a southward journey of about 1,200 miles.

The majority of North American species and a similar proportion of European birds take part in the great pageant of migration. In fact, more than a third of all the world's species are migratory to some degree and the numbers of individuals involved must run into the tens of billions. Migration is most pronounced in the Northern Hemisphere, where the much larger land masses are covered seasonally with winter's ice and snow. A considerable number of Eurasian and North American birds cross the equator to spend the winter deep in Africa or South America, but few land birds of the latter two continents reverse the process to pass their nonbreeding season in the Northern Hemisphere. They may journey northward toward the equator, and quite a number do, but the few that do cross it continue no great distance.

Among southern sea birds, however, there are several that do cross the equator to invade northern oceans. Wilson's petrel leaves its nesting grounds at the edge of the Antarctic Continent to forage in June, July and August as far north as the Newfoundland banks. Greater shearwaters from remote Tristan da Cunha in the South Atlantic and sooty shearwaters from islands around Cape Horn range to the offshore waters of Greenland. On the other side of the world the slender-billed shearwater, the "mutton bird" of the Australians, wanders in a great loop through the Pacific from the Bass Strait off southeast Australia past Japan to the Bering Sea and back again via the west coast of North America. The extraordinary thing is that the mob—millions of birds—is said to return to the same tiny islands on the same evening in late November.

MIGRATION is the greatest adventure in the life of a bird, the greatest risk it must take. Hundreds of millions of migrants never reach their destination. Birds do not have a built-in weather-forecasting system as some people naively believe, but seem to be triggered by the barometric pressure and other meteorological conditions prevailing at the start of their journey. They do not foresee the weather fronts, storms, winds or fogs they may meet along the way. Strong wind streams cutting across their axis of travel may carry them so far to sea at night that they may be unable to regain the land when they become aware of their plight in the morning. Fog seems to confuse their navigation and on misty nights lights attract them and they often crash into lighthouses, lighted monuments and high buildings. A hazard of man's air age that birds must now contend with are the ceilometers at airports and birds passing across these slender, vertically up-pointed beams sometimes plunge earthward. At Robins Air Force Base in Georgia it was estimated that 50,000 birds were killed in one night through the influence of a ceilometer beam. Television towers also take their toll: 20,000 migrants, mostly warblers, were killed in a single night at one tower, 1,000 feet high, in southern Wisconsin.

Natural catastrophes, however, far outweigh such man-made dangers. On the night of March 13 and 14, 1904, millions of Lapland longspurs, sparrowlike birds headed for their summer home in the arctic, were caught in a sticky snowstorm in southwestern Minnesota and northwestern Iowa. Confused, snow-laden and sodden, they crashed into buildings, wires and poles and onto the frozen ground. The ice of two small lakes, aggregating two square miles, was strewn with the bodies of 750,000 longspurs.

Hurricanes may carry sea birds as much as 2,000 miles from their home seas, to be dropped exhausted or dying on unfamiliar shores. Since the peak of the hurricane season coincides with the fall passage of many small migrants to the West Indies, a single storm might account for the loss of millions of lives. Ships entering the windless eye of a tropical storm have found the air full of small land birds which sought rest on the decks and rigging.

To collect some of the basic facts about migration, birdbanders in recent times have marked many millions of birds so that their flight could be followed and their destinations recorded. Although falconers had marked their hawks since medieval times so that they could be returned in case of loss, modern birdbanding did not begin until 1740, when Johann Leonhard Frisch of Berlin first tied red strings around the legs of swallows before the autumn migration. The first birdbander in America, appropriately, was John James Audubon. Two of the young phoebes on whose legs he had put silver threads returned the following year. A century later, in 1902, Paul Bartsch of Washington, D.C., attempted to mark birds in a scientific fashion by placing leg bands on night herons with the legend: "Return to Smithsonian Institution." One band was returned from Toronto, another from Cuba. In Europe, 12 years before Bartsch, Christian Mortensen, a Danish schoolmaster living in Viborg, had begun experimenting with zinc rings slipped around the legs of starlings.

Today banding (called "ringing" in Europe) is carried on extensively on all continents, including Antarctica. The United States and Canada, working in coordination, conduct the largest and most efficient operation. More than 2,000 banders in these countries mark approximately 600,000 birds every year. Over the years more than 13 million birds have been banded, with about one mil-

LONG-DISTANCE FLIERS

ARCTIC TERN

The maps on these two pages show the major itineraries of four well-known migratory birds. The greatest traveler of all, the arctic tern, leaves its northern colonies in late summer for the 10,000-mile trip to seas near Antarctica. Some pick a route through the Pacific, while others go by the west coast of Europe and Africa and may even stray to the Indian Ocean.

WHITE STORK

Storks summer in Europe but spend the winter in South Africa. Expert gliders, they prefer to ride rising air currents and will fly over water only if they can see land on the other side. Thus they have a problem crossing the Mediterranean. Most solve it by taking the eastern route through Asia Minor—then turning south into Africa. Others cross at Gibraltar.

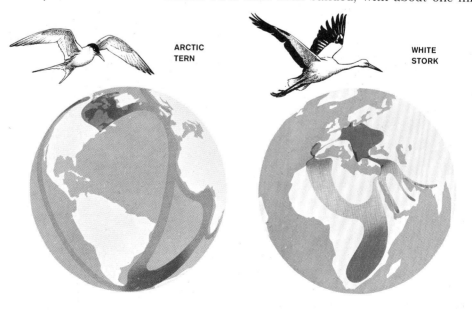

ARCTIC TERN

WHITE STORK

lion recoveries. To analyze this mass of information an electronic card index sorts IBM cards on which the information has been codified.

The U.S.S.R. has also banded three million birds and increases the score by more than 200,000 annually. In Germany the total number processed by three ornithological stations is now close to four million. The British Isles have ringed more than three million birds; Holland and Sweden more than one million each; Japan and Switzerland more than 500,000 each.

Young birds are easily banded before they leave the nest, but most banders prefer to work with adults. The devices for catching them are many. Perhaps the most elaborate is the Heligoland trap, basically a large camouflaged funnel of fine wire into which birds are driven via narrowing corridors to end up at last in a glass-backed collecting chamber. Somewhat similar is the Dutch decoy, a long wire funnel placed over a narrow stream into which inquisitive waterfowl are coaxed by a specially trained dog. In a more spectacular way, entire flocks of grazing geese are captured with great nets which are shot up and over them by explosive rockets released by remote control. Wary hawks are lured by decoy pigeons or owls and caught with automatic bow nets which snap shut over them, clamshell-fashion, when they strike. In fact, the banders have tried almost everything—hair-fine Japanese mist nets, drugged bait, jack lights, foot snares and a vast array of wire traps baited with food and water.

Some of the journeys documented by banding are extraordinary. An arctic tern banded as a flightless youngster by Oliver Austin Jr. on the coast of Labrador was picked up 90 days later on the coast of southeast Africa, 9,000 miles away. Another tern banded near Disko, Greenland, flew more than 10,000 miles to reach Durban in southeast Africa. Still another, ringed on the Arctic coast of Russia, was retaken off Australia, a distance of at least 14,000 miles.

There is no question that the arctic tern is the champion long-distance migrant. This streamer-tailed relative of the gulls which nests on the northernmost ice-free coasts flies to the edge of the antarctic and some individuals see more hours of daylight in a year than any other birds.

The golden plover is often cited as a close second for the marathon honors, traveling from the arctic tundra to the pampas of Argentina. The white-rumped sandpiper, however, makes the same fall sea hop from maritime Canada but does not stop in the latitude of the pampas—it continues for another 1,000 miles

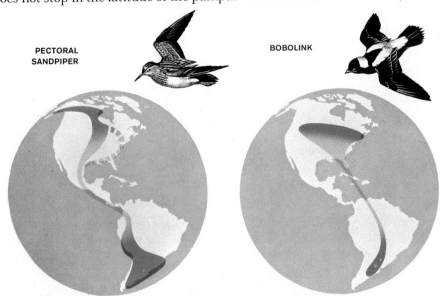

PECTORAL SANDPIPER

BOBOLINK

PECTORAL SANDPIPER

A shore bird that breeds in arctic tundra, the pectoral sandpiper does not lose sight of land as it migrates to its winter home in South America. The main route crosses the Great Plains, though in fall some birds make an arc that hits the Atlantic. This species has spread into Siberia, but the Asian birds still cross over into America before making their fall trip south.

BOBOLINK

A land bird that breeds in North American clover fields, the bobolink migrates to the grasslands of Argentina by island hopping through the Caribbean. The small bobolink colonies in the Northwest shun the most direct route to the south through Mexico; like the pectoral sandpipers in Siberia, they make a detour east to fly with their brothers along the ancestral flyway.

or more, often to the tip of Tierra del Fuego. Its associate, Baird's sandpiper, makes an equally long journey from the arctic via the high plains and the high Andes. Although their paths may be more than 2,000 miles apart, one over sea, the other through the interior, these two sandpipers often end their journey on the same Patagonian beaches.

Among land birds the bobolink has often been called the top migrant, covering 7,000 miles or more between the clover fields of Canada and the grasslands of Argentina. However, some barn swallows may travel up to even 9,000 miles, for the species breeds north to Alaska and some individuals reach southern Patagonia. Swallows from Scandinavia may rival their North American relatives by traveling the length of Europe and Africa, a flight of about 8,000 miles.

THE most spectacular of all migrants in Europe is the widely beloved white stork. Banding has shown that the westernmost population—birds of Holland, the Rhine and Spain—take a southwesterly path to the Strait of Gibraltar, where they ride the thermals to a great height before gliding the 10 miles over water to Africa. East of the Elbe River in Germany, storks take a southeasterly course and make an end run around the eastern Mediterranean to enter Egypt, following the Nile and then the Rift Valley all the way to South Africa to their wintering grounds. For a Danish stork this is a journey of 8,000 miles.

Although we often speak of "routes" and "flyways," there is probably not a single square mile of the earth's surface, excluding the polar icecaps, over which birds do not fly. A series of classic experiments made by George H. Lowery Jr. and Robert J. Newman while watching the night flight of birds through telescopes trained on the moon, as well as observations by radar workers, confirm without a doubt that most nocturnal migration of small land birds proceeds with the general air flow on a broad front—northward in the spring on warm air masses from the south, southward in the autumn on the cool winds of the north. The night migrants do not mass in flocks nor follow narrow paths. However, bird watchers observing migration at dawn see a startlingly different picture, particularly at coastal points. At daybreak, the birds, still moving, may be seen flying at an altitude from about 200 feet down to bush-top level and into the wind, as an airplane must do when it comes into the airfield. They are then often in groups and appear to be following definite paths, particularly when bodies of water, unseen at night, funnel them into peninsulas and islands. The field-glass birder often takes these concentration points to be normal "routes" and the disparity between what he sees and what the telescope or radar screen reveals has led to lively controversies over the nature of migration.

Although day migrants may be concentrated by such visual land contours as river valleys, coastlines and ridges, giving the impression that they are following precise routes, much diurnal migration also advances over a broad front. The "flyway" concept is an oversimplification, but the terminology is useful for the waterfowl administrators who, on the basis of the drainage pattern of the North American continent, distinguish between the Atlantic flyway, the Mississippi flyway, the Central flyway and the Pacific flyway. Actually many waterfowl switch from one flyway to another in their travels.

Diurnal migrants have a greater tendency to travel in flocks. Well-organized flocks of ducks, geese and swans (which also travel at night) swarm the continental flyways twice a year. Swallows travel by day in loose companies and assemble to roost at dusk. In the United States and Canada, red-winged blackbirds, grackles and starlings are mainly day migrants, as are robins, waxwings, goldfinches and many other familiar flocking species. Occasionally, however, some of these species may travel at night.

The first birds of spring in northern regions are mostly day migrants, following on the heels of retreating winter. Their times of arrival may vary two or three weeks from year to year. These birds (the American robin is typical) have been called "weather migrants," since it is the weather which apparently dominates their flights. Those that come later in the spring under the cover of darkness, the warblers and their associates, are much more precise in their times of arrival. They are often termed "instinct migrants," and weather, apart from wind, seems to have little effect on them.

Many species are only partially migratory. Bluebirds and many blue jays which breed in the northern United States and Canada travel southward to mingle in the southern states with resident bluebirds and blue jays which do not migrate at all. Similarly, in Europe most skylarks and wood larks migrate out of Scandinavia, but others stay throughout the year in England, where the seasons are more equable.

Migration, it must be pointed out, is not simply an expedient for escaping the cold. It is much more closely bound up with food, although some northern species pull out long before their food supply is diminished. Even many tropical birds migrate, but in most species the journeys are relatively short, regulated by the wet and the dry seasons or by the blooming and fruiting of certain plants.

Every autumn, between September and November, a few birds from North America turn up in Europe. Among these are not only strong-winged shore birds such as yellowlegs, dowitchers and pectoral, white-rumped and buff-breasted sandpipers, but also land birds such as cuckoos, thrushes, and warblers. For a long time it was thought that the frailer land birds might have hitchhiked on boats. But though assisted passages on boats have been recorded—a white-throated sparrow aboard a liner outbound from New York once hitched a ride all the way to the Scilly Isles—a better explanation is that they were borne over by violent winds, or it has even been suggested that they may have been caught at high altitudes in the jet streams, the powerful winds that sweep from west to east around the globe.

FLIGHT speeds of birds have been clocked many times, but usually at ground speed, and it has been asserted that migrating birds travel faster than they do at other times. The speed of most small birds seldom exceeds 30 miles per hour, although swallows and particularly starlings are much faster. Migrating hawks cruise along at 30 to 40 miles per hour. Most shore birds average between 40 and 50 miles per hour, while many ducks travel at 50 to 60.

At such speeds migrating birds may cover several hundreds of miles in a day or a night. It is routine for North American migrants to do more than 500 miles nonstop across the Gulf of Mexico, where there are no midway islands. A turnstone, one of a cosmopolitan species of shore bird banded in Germany, covered 510 miles in 25 hours. Blue geese make the 1,700 miles from James Bay in Canada to coastal Louisiana in 60 hours.

Most routine migration probably takes place within 3,000 feet of the earth, although David Lack, computing the altitude of British night migrants with radar, found that some small land birds often travel at 5,000 feet and may sometimes go as high as 14,000 feet. Radar has recorded birds at altitudes of 20,000 feet, perhaps not too surprising since many species cross both the Andes and the Himalayas during migration.

NAVIGATION BY THE SUN

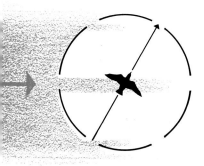

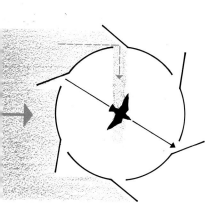

To test the possibility that birds used the sun as a compass during migration, Gustav Kramer experimented with starlings during their periods of migratory restlessness. When he caged them in an experimental aviary that was lighted only by the sun (top), he found that the birds fluttered about and soon aligned themselves in the same directions of the compass they would have followed had they been free. But when he used adjustable mirrors to deflect the natural sunlight by 90 degrees, the starlings changed their direction to precisely the same degree.

What started migration? Students of the question, noting that the birds of the Northern Hemisphere are the most migratory, have suggested that the ice sheets during the Pleistocene epoch might have been originally responsible. Birds were forced south ahead of the advancing glaciers, according to this theory, and followed them back when they receded. Each winter is now like a brief recurrence of the ice age, with the birds retreating to their ancestral haven and returning when the snow and ice have gone. The idea sounds plausible, but it does not explain migration in many parts of the world that were never touched by glaciation. Consequently most ornithologists now reject this theory as a basic cause of migration, believing rather that it must have been going on for many millions of years, not just the last one or two million years spanned by the Pleistocene.

There is no question that the process has been an evolutionary one: birds originating in warm climates probably spread outward in their search for food. Many found it in abundance in higher latitudes but were forced to withdraw when winter came. Although many of the adventurers perished, natural selection has favored the survival of the more flexible individuals. The wheatear, a small Old World thrush which spends the winter in Africa, has ventured across the North Atlantic via the British Isles and Iceland to colonize Greenland and Labrador. It has also extended its range from Asia across the Bering Sea into Alaska. But when it migrates it leaves North America entirely, the Labrador birds retracing their path eastward across the North Atlantic and the Alaskan birds westward across the Bering Sea to return to their ancestral African home.

THE *remote* causes of migration and the evolution of the habit are quite distinct from the *immediate* causes. What prompts birds to start their migration at approximately the same time each year—what internal clock or what external stimuli? We know that the endocrine glands, the controls that make male birds sing and females lay eggs, undergo great changes before the nesting season. There are other changes after the nesting season is over. It is during these periods that most birds migrate. And we know, too, that one of the forces that seems to start these changes is light—the increase of light in the spring and the decrease of light in the fall. When the right day comes, the bird, not thinking how or why, leaves for its distant goal.

The factors that initiate migration are so complex as to be the despair of analysts. The annual stimulus may be reflected in the state of the gonads in some species, but not in others. Some birds build up a fat reserve, others do not. Light and meteorological conditions seem to trigger migration in some birds but not in others.

Birds have extraordinary stamina to travel the distances they do; no creatures on earth are more athletic. To survive the aerial life requires Olympic standards of fitness. Long-distance migrants have the ability to store a vast fuel supply in the form of fat, sometimes doubling their weight. But the aspect of migration that elicits the greatest wonder is the manner in which birds find their way— their navigation. Just how do they direct themselves over unknown country?

A large percentage of all bird migrants travel at night when they cannot easily make use of landmarks. However, some waterfowl, geese in particular, are thought to benefit by a tradition of paths taken in years past by existing members of the flock, a visual memory of stopping places which might not be in a straight line. How else can we explain such journeys as that of the European white stork, or of the Ross's goose which, migrating southward through the

North American plains, makes an abrupt westward turn in the vicinity of Great Falls, Montana, to cross the Rockies?

What about those birds that cross great stretches of ocean to remote islands without the benefit of sextant or compass? There are no "sea marks" for them to follow. We marvel at the golden plovers that make their way unerringly across 2,000 miles or more of open ocean from Alaska to the Hawaiian Islands and at the bristle-thighed curlews that travel from coastal Alaska to Tahiti and other islands as much as 6,000 miles away. Many are young birds making their first journey without the guidance of adults. The young bronze cuckoo of New Zealand, after being raised by foster parents which themselves do not migrate, navigates northward 2,500 miles over the open sea to the Solomon and Bismarck Islands for its first winter. Another New Zealand species, the long-tailed cuckoo, travels up to 4,000 miles to outlying Pacific islands.

The term "homing," almost self-explanatory, may be defined as the return to a goal. This may take the bird over unknown territory and, unlike an invisible rubber band that has been snapped, it may not be a direct return; migrating birds seldom travel in a straight line. Migrants from Scandinavia bound for the Low Countries or France are often drifted by winds to British shores, or even to the Shetland Islands of Scotland.

It must be kept in mind that the wind, unless it is turbulent or gusty, does not *blow* a bird or push it. The bird is borne like a swimmer in a current of water. It can seldom travel "as the crow flies," but may log hundreds of extra miles as it makes up for the effects of wind drift before reaching its ultimate destination.

Birds have been put to the experiment hundreds of times to test their homing abilities over unknown terrain. Most of them never were seen again, but some achieved notable records. A European swift transported 155 miles got back to where it belonged in four hours. A Laysan albatross released 3,200 miles from its home on Midway Island in the central Pacific returned within 10 days. A male Manx shearwater removed to Boston's Logan International Airport flew 3,050 miles back across the Atlantic, arriving at its burrow on Skokholm Island off Wales 12½ days later.

CRITICS have suggested that perhaps birds are able to record in some way all the twists and turns made by the vehicle that transported them and that, returning, they simply retrace these twists and turns. To put this to the test, two cages of starlings were dispatched by train from a German village to Berlin, 93 miles away. One cage was put on a phonograph turntable that revolved 5,000 times during the journey. This would require remembering all 5,000 revolutions plus the turns of the railroad track. Yet when released in Berlin these birds returned home as quickly as those in the other cage. Even more conclusive results were obtained in England when pigeons were transported in lightproof drums that rotated erratically.

Students of migration have also advanced the idea that birds are sensitive to the earth's magnetic field and may be able to measure it. It has further been suggested that their inner ear reacts to the Coriolis effect, the mechanical effect produced by the rotation of the earth. Dr. Henry L. Yeagley, utilizing both these ideas, engaged in elaborate experiments to prove that birds sense their position by the combined effect of the Coriolis effect and the earth's magnetic field—but although the concept seemed to hold promise, it could not be proved.

The late Gustav Kramer of Germany brilliantly showed that birds which travel by day orient themselves by the position of the sun. Working with starlings

AND BY THE STARS

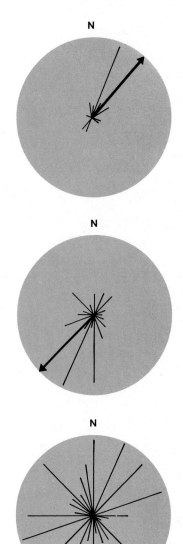

By placing warblers in a planetarium during their spring restlessness, E.G.F. Sauer found that night migrants use stars for guidance. When he shone a spring sky on the ceiling the birds faced northwest (top), the direction in which they would normally migrate. When he twisted the star pattern the birds turned too. An autumn experiment (center) gave similar results. But with no stars as guides (bottom) birds faced in all directions. The short lines in these circles indicate movement by a few birds, longer lines by more birds, thick arrows by most of the birds.

in an elaborate circular contraption with six evenly spaced windows, each revealing a patch of sky, he found that during their migratory restlessness these birds perched with their bodies pointed in the direction they would fly if migrating, i.e., northeast in spring and southwest in fall. He then decided to find out if he could trick the birds into facing in another direction by "moving" the sun. He did this by putting adjustable mirrors outside the windows of the cage. The sunlight was reflected into the cage at a different angle and the birds promptly lined themselves up in accordance with this new position of the sun. On the other hand, on cloudy days when the birds could not see the sun at all, they were unable to align themselves properly.

Although this all sounded most significant, it failed to take into account one very important fact: the sun does not stay in the same place in the sky during the day, nor does it even appear in the same place on different days. Was it possible that the birds could make allowances for this? Kramer decided to find out. He built a circular cage and around the inside he placed a number of small feeding dishes. Then he put a starling in the cage and soon taught it to locate a particular dish with food in it according to the direction from which the sun was shining from outside the cage. This was done at a certain hour each day, and when the starling was thoroughly trained it was then tested at a different hour. It still went to the right dish, apparently able to compensate for the changing angle of the sun.

REVEALING as these experiments were, they said nothing about how birds navigate at night. It fell to the genius of another young German, E.F.G. Sauer, to propose that nocturnal migrants apparently take their direction from the constellations of the stars. Sauer used a round cage with a clear plexiglass top that permitted a direct view of the night sky. The birds appeared to orient themselves by the stars and as soon as clouds hid them they became bewildered. Later Sauer exposed the birds to an artificial night sky in the planetarium at the Mariners' School in Bremen. The cage of birds was so placed in the planetarium that only the dome, 20 feet in diameter, was visible. The birds took their directions from the stars and were easily duped when the constellations in the artificial heavens were shifted.

Although there is increasing evidence that birds use celestial navigation in establishing the main direction of their travel, it still remains a mystery how they pinpoint their goals. In addition to radar, there have been numerous setups employed to obtain more precise information about navigation. Automatic devices have been used in a wide range of experiments concerned with migratory restlessness and orientation as displayed by caged migrants. Mallards and other birds released at night have been furnished with tiny flashlights and miniature radio transmitters, enabling the student to keep track of their whereabouts, and apparatus has been devised to record the tiny voices of migrants high in the night sky. Massive capture of migrants by means of mist nets at various coastal points and open-sky watching are among the techniques used currently by the student of migration.

During recent years we have been accumulating data at an increasing pace, but the tantalizing thing is that these data are often so contradictory that they yield no clear answers. As Robert Newman points out: "The history of homing studies has been that no sooner is a hypothesis erected, purporting to explain all the assembled evidence, than new evidence is found to demolish it." It will be up to the bright, young biologists of the future to clarify the age-old riddle.

A REED BUNTING IS HELD GENTLY BUT FIRMLY IN A MIST NET, HAVING BLUNDERED INTO ITS SILKEN MESH BEFORE REALIZING IT WAS THERE

Mysterious Voyagers

Spring and fall, for longer than recorded time, men have looked up in wonder as clouds of migrating birds darkened the skies. To learn where birds go during these mysterious journeys, men have observed them with binoculars, telescopes, radar and other aircraft tracking devices. In addition, they have brought birds to earth in nets, banded them, and sometimes even daubed them with dye.

RESPONSE TO LIGHT in a feeding experiment indicates that birds orient themselves to a light source. This starling, circled by small food boxes in a cage, quickly learned to face toward a bright movable light to find the box that contained its food. Experimenters reason that a similar response to the sun can be useful to migrating birds in orienting themselves as they fly.

How Birds Find Their Way

How birds can find their way with apparent ease over vast distances remains the unsolved riddle of migration. So precisely can they follow their invisible paths that scientists have from time to time suspected that birds possess a special sense unknown to man. At one time they were thought to have a kinesthetic sense, by which they could form patterns of their route through pressures on the inner ear. Another idea was that birds navigate through responses to the earth's magnetic field, perhaps even to its rotational effects. None of these hypotheses has, however, stood the test of experiment.

More convincing is the evidence that the bird's vision plays the primary role in its sense of direction and position. And if the bird locates itself by means of visual landmarks like river valleys or mountains, it is only a step further to the idea advanced by Gustav Kramer and others that a bird might be able to use the sun as a compass and even have a time sense which enables it to adjust its course to compensate for the sun's movement across the sky.

MOVABLE MIRRORS can beam sunlight into this experimental aviary at odd angles, making birds inside act as if the sun is in different positions. The birds adjust themselves accordingly.

A HOMING EXPERIMENT from an aviary in an excavation reveals the importance to carrier pigeons of vision in navigation. Birds raised here were below ground level and could never orient themselves with a look at the horizon. When they were taken a few miles away and released, they could not find their way back. Birds raised above ground had less trouble homing.

A BOOM NET, so named because it is arched into the air by explosives, is laid on the ground in folds.

Grounded Geese

Nets and snares have long been used to catch birds for the pot and the headdress. Only recently have they been used to help study the movements of birds, which are freed as soon as they have been trapped and banded. Among the most ingenious of the new devices is the Japanese mist net shown on page 109. Spun of almost invisible dark thread and strung near the ground on poles, it enmeshes small woodland species which would escape most wire traps. Large game birds may be taken in boom nets like the one seen here.

SHOOTING HIGH, the net is spread out by metal weights and soars over a flock of Canada geese.

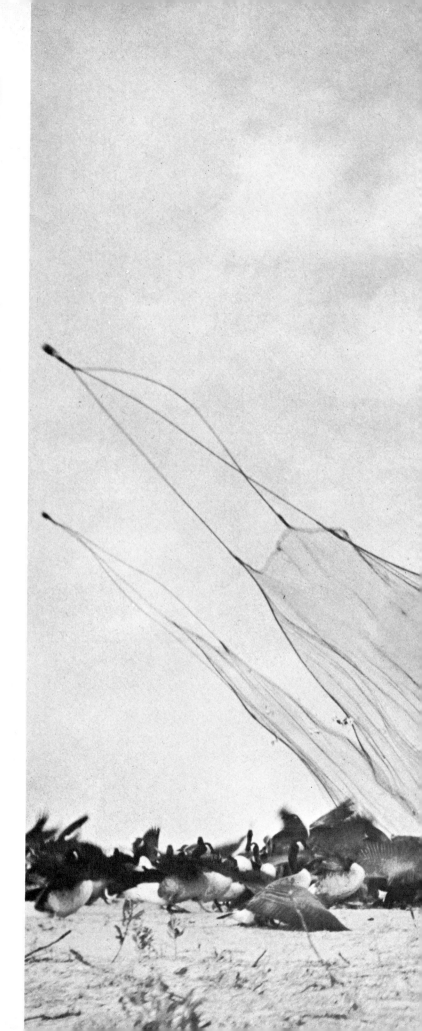

NETTED GEESE await transfer to wire cages by wildlife agents at a North Carolina game refuge.

BIRDS ARE LIFTED from cages to record their age, weight and sex and, finally, fitted with bands.

A BANDED GOOSE flies free. When releasing birds, banders prefer to let whole families go together.

YOUNG SIBERIAN JAYS, adapted to the cold, huddle together for warmth in an early frost. These nonmigrants are more thickly feathered than their migrating kin and by fluffing out their plumage can further insulate themselves, trapping their own body heat. Thus they do not need to escape the cold, but if food becomes scarce, they may fly as far as central Europe to seek it.

ALUMINUM BANDS developed by the U.S. Fish and Wildlife Service come in 14 diameters, from 0.083 to 0.875 inches, to fit birds of many sizes.

The Telltale Band

Of all the ways men have devised for following birds, the simplest and the most effective is the process of banding, which picks out a single bird at two specific moments: first when the band is snapped around its shank, and again when it is once more recovered, alive or dead.

More than half of the 600,000 birds banded in North America each year are small songbirds tagged by dedicated amateurs. Waterfowl and other game birds are usually banded by government professionals. Although game birds are less than half of the total, they account for a disproportionate 90 per cent of all recoveries—many sent in by sportsmen who have found bands on birds they have shot.

Bands have yielded amazing records, such as that of a lesser yellowlegs which flew 1,900 miles from Cape Cod to Martinique in six days; or the oystercatcher, banded in 1929 in the Netherlands, which turned up healthy 28 years later. But most important is the fact that the data from the million or so birdbands turned in during the last 60 years has led to new knowledge about the travels, population dynamics and survival of many species, and thus to better laws to protect them.

A BAND IS ATTACHED to the leg of a pintail duck as it lies quietly in the arms of a wildlife agent. About 45,000 pintails are now banded annually.

TAGGING SNOW GEESE, agents take bands from a spiked stand on which they are stacked for quick use. Bands are marked with a serial number and the U.S. Fish and Wildlife Service address to which the band should be mailed.

Fancy Dress for Science

The most startling innovation in tracking birds is the gaudy device of dyeing them with bright colors. First used systematically in 1955 by the California Fish and Game Department to follow the northward flight of geese, this new technique immediately proved its value in bringing quick results as incredulous observers phoned in tales of pink, green and yellow geese all the way up to the Arctic Ocean.

As spectacular as the dyeing method is, it has its limitations. Because all birds molt, the dyed feathers are bound to be shed within a season. Nonetheless, the information to be gained from it can be useful in determining the behavior of local populations. In Boston, for example, dyeing was employed to check the movements of the clouds of gulls around nearby Logan International Airport, where they were a constant menace to aircraft. The study revealed that the birds were attracted by adjacent garbage dumps and by fishing fleets; control these and the airport menace might be reduced.

FRESHLY SPRAYED, a bright-hued gull lands among its pristine fellows. Although they look bizarre to humans, other gulls apparently see nothing odd in the dyed birds.

A RELUCTANT VICTIM, this herring gull is squirted with a scarlet spray in a project to ascertain the habits and range of gulls from six colonies along the New England coast.

6

How Birds Communicate

Most birds seem to enjoy each others' company. There are exceptions, of course—loners like the birds of prey, herons (when they are not nesting), grouse, rails, cuckoos, nightjars, kingfishers, dippers and some of the birds of tropical forests. But the large majority of bird species are social. Doing things together requires a language, a means of communication. Birds have a variety of ways of sending messages—by voice, by action and by display of plumage or adornment: devices and symbols by which they talk to each other.

Understanding this "language" has long fired the imaginations of scientists and laymen. King Solomon, the wisest of men, reputedly could talk to the birds and the beasts with the aid of a magic ring. Today, behaviorists like Konrad Lorenz of the Max Planck Institute in Germany, Niko Tinbergen of the Department of Zoology at Oxford University in England and Daniel Lehrman of Rutgers University in the United States are remarkably close to really understanding the ways of birds. None of these authorities, however, would be so brash as to assert he could translate avian language directly into human speech. For although they agree that birds are capable of limited learning, they are bound to point out that much of their "language" is innate, unlike human language which must be learned. The communication of birds is far removed from anything like the spoken word; it is more a matter of inborn mechanisms, some of which are termed "releasers," "imprinting," and "displacement." These will be described in detail further on.

Why do birds sing and what is the function of song? First, we must distinguish song from call notes and the other sounds that birds make. Olin Sewall Pettingill, director of the Laboratory of Ornithology at Cornell, offers this definition of bird song: "A series of sounds consistently repeated according to some specific pattern and produced, as a rule, mainly by males and usually during the breeding season." By avoiding the word "vocal" this definition includes the rhythmic tapping of woodpeckers, the drumming of grouse with their wings and the aerial performances of woodcock and snipe, in which the sounds are produced by notched feathers of the wings and tail.

BIRD-SONG NOTATION

Below are three different ways of transcribing the song of a bird—in this case, the eastern meadowlark. The first one, ordinary musical notation, can give only a rough approximation because birds do not restrict their musical vocabularies to our customary notes, intervals and tempos. The second, a musical shorthand system devised by Aretas A. Saunders, still depends upon the human ear, with its limitation in perceiving extra-high notes, tiny pauses, and very rapid trills. It required the development of the tape recorder and the oscillograph to make possible a scientifically accurate system of notation. Together, the two devices can produce a permanent record (bottom), called an audiospectrogram, which will show pitch (in kilocycles per second), volume (by thickness of line) and tempo.

Although they differ in detail and in technique, all three notations have the same general form: a pair of descending phrases of almost equal length, with the first pitched slightly higher than the second.

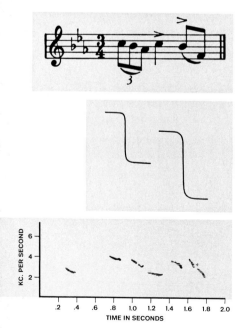

Some bird songs are so elaborate as to fall on the ears like phrases of divine music. The thrushes as a family are perhaps the most gifted of all singers. Certain other bird voices are discordant, insectlike or staccato—anything but musical. But whether the bird is a Henslow's sparrow in an Ohio meadow hiccuping its monotonous *tsi-lick* or a slate-backed solitaire in a Mexican cloud forest making all other singers sound like amateurs, the meaning in the vast majority of songs is always essentially the same: a call, first of all, from male to male, proclaiming territory and warning other males away, and secondarily to females, advertising his maleness to any available prospective mate if he is not already committed. The sentimentalist who likes to think that avian melodies are hymns of joy finds it hard to believe that they are generally an announcement of status—tough talk to rivals. Singing becomes more frequent, more aggressive, when another male is within hearing. Should the interloper cross the invisible line that defines the territory, he is attacked, but usually a song is enough to send him on his way.

Even a badly stuffed male specimen planted within the domain of a singing male will be attacked, particularly if attention is drawn to it with a sound recording. But a robin will not attack a stuffed sparrow, wren or blackbird. It reacts only to other robins. David Lack of the Edward Grey Institute at Oxford, experimenting with England's little robin redbreast, discovered that the thing that made it "see red" was the red breast of its opponent. Even a tuft of red breast feathers on a wire was violently attacked. When that was removed the bird attacked the space where it had been. In North America the red "epaulets" of a singing red-winged blackbird are puffed out when it threatens a rival. Similarly, in Europe, the white shoulder patches of the familiar chaffinch are its battle banners. Bold patterns, colors and other adornment act as "releasers," evoking the fighting response in other red-blooded males while sowing the seeds of submission in females ready to mate. Aggression and counteraggression have brought bird song and bird plumage to its high degree of evolution; were it not for this fact of life, birds would lack much of their glamour.

If a stuffed male will trigger an attack it is hardly surprising that a stuffed female will often elicit an equally appropriate reaction. That she may seem frigid seems to matter little. As long as she is readily identifiable as a female of the species, she is desirable and the deluded male may return again and again to copulate. Brewer's blackbirds (even ones with mates) will actually try out headless and wingless specimens of the opposite sex.

William Vogt, testing the emotions of a male yellowthroat, changed the apparent sex of a stuffed female by pasting a black mask across its face (the male yellowthroat has this mask, the female lacks it). When the male returned, its first reaction, according to Vogt, seemed to be one of shocked surprise, "as though its mistress had betrayed it"; then it attacked the deceiver.

Threat, as Tinbergen points out, is in many species the first phase of courtship. When a female is attracted to a male by his song he may intimidate her at first. But she may disarm him by some sign of appeasement, some subtle gesture such as turning the head away (the standard procedure of the black-headed gull), or she may express submission by acting like a baby, quivering her wings and begging to be fed. So what does the male do? He feeds her. Courtship feeding is common in many songbirds, a sort of avian baby talk that leads inevitably to mating.

Song plays its part here too. While proclamation of territory is its primary function, it undoubtedly also strengthens the bond between the pair during the short season of nesting. The term "emotional song" has been used to explain away those forms of singing that do not seem to have anything to do with territory—the whisper songs of autumn, occasional winter singing and such ecstatic outpourings as the night song of the ovenbird which so intrigued Thoreau at Walden Pond.

Singing is most persistent early in the morning and may taper off by midday. Thrushes sing most eloquently just before dusk. Perhaps the most tireless (or should we say tiresome) of all birds in the deciduous woodlands of eastern North America is the red-eyed vireo, which has been called the "preacher bird" because of the monotonous repetition of its phrases. The indefatigable Louise de Kiriline Lawrence reports that one male red-eyed vireo repeated this refrain 22,197 times between dawn and dark, a record not likely to be challenged except by another red-eyed vireo.

Bᴵᴿᴰˢ that do not look alike may sometimes have rather similar songs—a junco and a pine warbler, for example. But it is axiomatic that birds of very similar appearance invariably have distinctive songs. There are many small fly-catchers in the Americas, leaf warblers in Europe and birds of the nightjar-whippoorwill tribe throughout the world which look so much alike that they confound the experts until they speak. Song is the isolating mechanism which prevents these birds from making mistakes in choosing partners.

It seems to be a rule of thumb that modestly colored birds are among the most gifted singers. There is perhaps a good reason for this: whereas brightly colored birds tend to use their gay patterns to advertise themselves, many of the drab, streaky birds of the fields and plains can only advertise vocally. Lacking bright feathers and quite lost in a big landscape, they climb into the sky to pour out their song. The skylark, colorless on the ground, dominates many acres of meadow from its aerial vantage point, showering down a tireless torrent of music.

Is song innate or acquired? Some birds, raised artificially from the egg without a chance to hear their own kind, instinctively sing as they should when they reach the proper age. It is quite likely that most species with unvarying song patterns, the chipping sparrow, for example, or the least flycatcher, would not have to learn their songs even if they were raised in soundproof chambers. But certain other more gifted musicians, such as nightingales and mockingbirds, must learn their art from older birds, even though as untutored youngsters they may have a song of a sort, formless but apparently innate.

WHAT'S IN A NAME

The whippoorwill, the bobwhite and numerous other birds get their names from the sounds people hear them making. What people hear birds saying, however, depends very much on what country they live in. An interesting example is the list below of the various interpretations of the call of the chiffchaff, taken from the different translations of a "Field Guide to the Birds of Britain and Europe."

Eɴɢʟɪsʜ: chiff, chaff, chiff, chiff, chaff
Fɪɴɴɪsʜ: til, tal, til, til, tal
Gᴇʀᴍᴀɴ: zilp, zalp, zilp, zilp, zalp
Fʀᴇɴᴄʜ: tyip, tsyep, tyip, tyip, tsyep
Dᴜᴛᴄʜ: tjif, tjaf, tjif, tjif, tjaf
Sᴡᴇᴅɪsʜ: tji, tju, tji, tji, tju
Sᴘᴀɴɪsʜ: sib, sab, sib, sib, sab
Iᴛᴀʟɪᴀɴ: ciff, ciaff, ciff, ciff, ciaff
Iᴄᴇʟᴀɴᴅɪᴄ: tsjiff, tsjaff, tsjiff, tsjiff, tsjaff
Dᴀɴɪsʜ: tjif, tjaf, tjif, tjif, tjaf

Mimicry is undoubtedly acquired. The introduced starling, which often mimics the wood peewee, killdeer and meadowlark in New England, never makes these sounds in Old England, the land of its origin. Mockingbirds in California specialize in imitations of California tree frogs, California woodpeckers and scrub jays, whereas mockingbirds in Kentucky or Maryland who do not hear these sounds never include them in their repertoire.

Before the days of modern tape recorders the gifted analyst of bird songs Aretas Saunders devised a system of symbols to record and interpret them visually. Relying on this system and his exceptional ear he discovered that in many species no two individuals sang exactly alike. Over a period of years, he recorded 884 variations in the song of the song sparrow. Some years later Donald J. Borror pursued the matter further with a tape recorder. Concentrating on one male song sparrow at Hog Island, Maine, he recorded its song 462 times and on analysis found that there were 13 distinct song patterns and 187 minor variations. However, the basic quality was always the same and each song was instantly recognizable as that of a song sparrow.

It is quite likely that differences between the voices of individuals, scarcely discernible to our ear, do help birds to recognize their neighbors and detect strangers. Richard L. Penney discovered that an Adélie penguin in its crowded antarctic rookery could recognize its mate by voice when it returned after an absence of months. Penguin chicks also responded to their parents' voices when they were played back on a tape recorder.

TAPE recorders have revolutionized the study of bird voice. These instruments make it possible not only to compare call notes and songs critically but also, by putting the tapes through an oscillograph or a spectrograph, to analyze them visually. In fact, during the last 10 or 15 years the new science of bio-acoustics has revealed more about the classification of bird voices, their meaning and their individual development, or ontogeny, than had been found out in all the preceding centuries. In North America, the Cornell University Laboratory of Ornithology at Ithaca, New York, is the clearing house for bird recordings of all continents. More than 15,000 recordings are now in its fast-growing collection. The British Broadcasting Corporation has a large collection and similar work is carried on in Sweden.

The various sounds that birds make have been grouped by Nicholas Collias of the University of California into five main categories: (1) flocking and group movements; (2) food; (3) predators and enemies; (4) parent-young relationships; and (5) sexual behavior and related aggression. Song, of course, falls predominantly into the last category.

Migrating birds often utter special contact notes. Some of the sounds heard in the night sky, especially certain notes of low intensity, are a puzzle even to the expert, who must conclude, since he hears them only at night, that their special function is to communicate when birds cannot see each other. However, some families of North American birds—the wood warblers, the sparrows and the thrushes—are vocal during their nocturnal passage, while others apparently are not. The vireos, tyrant flycatchers and tanagers, all of which travel at night, seem to be silent.

The familiar quail of eastern North America has in addition to its well-enunciated *bob-white!* a "covey call," a querulous *ka-loi-kee?*, which is answered by a similar *whoil-kee!* This cry of the adult which brings the scattered flock together is believed to evolve from the peeping "lost" signal of the baby chicks.

Many flocking birds have their special feeding notes, assembly signals and flight calls. On the stubble fields where they graze, Canada geese converse in low, grunting notes. Loud honking cries signal the take-off and as the long, organized wedge passes toward the horizon the flock keeps up the stirring chorus.

Every bird has a vocabulary dealing with its most urgent preoccupation—food. Familiar to every farmyard is the brooding hen's excited food call that brings her scattered chicks on the double. A young robin, having finished off a worm or two brought by its parents, may not make a sound for a while, but when hunger begins to reassert itself the youngster starts to utter light peeps which give way to a louder note and finally to a two-syllabled call. These notes, becoming more insistent, help the parents locate the fledgling if it has left the nest. When they finally arrive with the next meal, the youngster gives a little breathless cry that can only be interpreted as anticipation.

A herring gull finding a small amount of food wolfs it down in silence, but should there be more than it can manage alone it proclaims its good fortune to every other gull within hearing with a three-syllabled cry. Similarly, parrots and other fruit-eating birds, as has been noted in Chapter 3, loudly inform their neighbors of a bonanza.

It may be that more cooperation exists among feeding birds than is recognized. In northern parts of Europe and America, woodland birds—titmice, chickadees, woodpeckers, nuthatches, tree creepers, kinglets, etc.—often hunt in mixed groups. Similar mixed flocks roam the tropical forests. It is quite likely that the various species recognize each others' calls—the starting notes, stopping notes, assembly calls, food calls and warning cries—much as an English-speaking person might in time recognize basic meanings in French, German or Spanish without being able really to speak the language.

Though birds may cooperate, more often they compete for food. At a crowded feeding board they may threaten each other by voice or posture. A chickadee or a grosbeak gapes aggressively with open bill, an irritated nuthatch spreads its wings and tail. One bird outbluffs the other; actual fights are rare.

Warning cries may distinguish whether the menace is a hawk in the air or a dog, a cat or a man on the ground. A hen, spotting a hawk, has a harsh scream that sends her chicks into hiding, but when a dog or a man approaches the alarm is a cackle.

Chickadees, when momentarily alarmed, sound a sharp chattering note that sends all nearby birds to cover, but the discovery of a small owl will elicit a distinctive, persistent and complaining call. Joseph Grinnell in California noted that a flock of bush tits, harassed by a small hawk, united in a shrill, quavering chorus which lasted for as much as two minutes and which made it quite impossible to isolate any one bird by sound.

The biologists Hubert and Mabel Frings and their collaborators, experimenting with tape recordings, found that they could attract a crowd of cawing crows within six minutes by loudly playing the rallying call that crows give when they see an owl. On the other hand, herring gulls fled from garbage dumps when their alarm calls were played back, and starlings abandoned their roosts for a time, until they apparently sensed that the alarm was a false one.

A bird of prey means sudden death to many lesser birds, but there has been some evidence that even young birds that have had no experience with aerial predators scurry to cover at the sight of one. Geese, whose only masters are large eagles, are sometimes put to flight by distant planes which, like eagles,

HAWK OR GOOSE?

HAWK

DUMMY

GOOSE

To test how birds react to shape and movement in avoiding danger from the skies, an ingenious experiment was conducted. A dummy silhouette was constructed, midway in shape between a predator hawk and a harmless goose. When the dummy was towed through the air in one direction, it apparently resembled a long-necked goose, and chicks on the ground ignored it. But when it was towed in the other direction, the chicks froze in terror. Some scientists contend that the chicks, which had never seen hawks before, were reacting instinctively to the shape of the enemy bird of prey. Others believe that the chicks cringed not because they recognized a predator's silhouette but only because they feared an unfamiliar shape.

seem to move slowly for their size. Tinbergen and Lorenz, employing pasteboard cutouts pulled along an overhead wire, concluded that a short-necked or neckless silhouette with a long tail meant hawk, whereas a long neck and short tail meant some harmless water bird. They made an all-purpose model, a pair of wings with a long projection on one side, a short one on the other. By pulling it short end forward they sent ducks and goslings into a panic; pulling it the other way left them unconcerned.

Some birds are so similar in appearance—like male and female terns with their identical black caps and red bills—that they must have some device by which to tell each other apart. The male tern makes himself known by presenting a small fish, as one would offer a box of flowers or an engagement ring. The two birds then fly ceremoniously over the colony, passing the symbolic gift back and forth. The crucial test comes when the male, settled on his territory, presents the fish once more. If it is accepted properly and the other bird submits to his pecks there is no doubt it is a female and a likely partner. But if it is another male he will refuse to submit to intimidation; if the interloper does not quickly fly away, a beak-to-beak grapple follows.

Male herons also have the problem of selecting mates from a crowd of birds which look exactly alike. Each species has a ceremonial display shared by no other heron. The night heron, for instance, goes through a "song and dance" on the nest site, extending his neck forward while treading with his feet. Then he spreads his plumes, drops his head almost to the level of his feet and utters a short *plup-buzz*. This bizarre performance attracts amenable females, which at first are driven off, but finally a lucky spouse is allowed to enter the nest platform—provided her legs are bright pink, a sign of full readiness to mate. This ritual is as ancient and unvaried as the dynasty of night herons itself; should any of its steps be omitted mating is not consummated.

IN some birds reciprocal greeting ceremonies help keep the bond between the pair strong. European white storks are practically mute, but a castanetlike rattling of the bill, audible for half a mile, serves them for communication. When the bird on the nest spots its mate winging homeward it rattles, flinging its head backward until it touches the back, then throwing it forward in a stiff bow. The arriving bird joins in the display and they clatter in unison, tossing their heads, bowing and pirouetting with cocked tails and half-spread wings.

Like the storks, many other water birds continue their reciprocal displays even after the family of growing young demands their attention. Gannets stretch their necks and cross their beaks, reasserting their loyalty to each other.

Bird display, like song, may be an aggressive act aimed primarily at rival males. Wild turkey gobblers on promenade pay more attention to each other than to the hens. Shoulder to shoulder the big toms strut, their erect tails fully fanned and their stiff wing-quills dragging the ground. In the fever pitch of their rivalry their naked heads turn bright blue and their wattles become gorged with blood; when one bird gobbles they all gobble simultaneously. When a hen is ready to mate she must take the initiative, literally prostrating herself before the tom turkey of her choice before he will allow himself to be diverted from his self-centered pomposity.

Arena behavior, in which the males parade and perform on a chosen piece of ground, is a highly specialized form of bird courtship in which the successful males are polygynous and the females are promiscuous. Furthermore, it is usually the female that chooses the mate. No lasting ties are formed and the males assume no nesting responsibilities. A number of grouse and other fowl-like birds have arenas where the cocks gather, and a variety of tropical birds are also known to hold court in forest arenas: the peacocklike argus pheasant of Asia, the birds of paradise of New Guinea, the bright orange cock-of-the-rock of South American mountains, the tiny manakins of tropical America and some hummingbirds. Jackson's dancing whydah of the East African grasslands may have an arena with as many as 100 individual dancing territories, each with a ring of trampled grass encircling a central tuft around which a male dances (the tuft perhaps represents a symbolic nest).

ONE is led to ponder the biological advantages of the arena system. The late E. Thomas Gilliard of The American Museum of Natural History pointed out that such polygynous habits make it possible for a very small percentage of the males to perpetuate the species. One of the most fantastic of the arena birds, for instance, is the sage grouse of western North America. A large arena may be as much as half a mile long and 200 yards wide with 400 cocks stationed 25 to 40 feet apart. Until recently, many ranchmen believed that sage grouse did not mate as other birds do but that the cocks spawn and the hens pick up the spawn. But researches of James Simon and John Scott in Wyoming revealed that the flock, displaying and fighting every morning during a period of weeks, gradually establishes a hierarchy, with the most vigorous cock, the one most ready to strut and fight, occupying the key position. The remarkable discovery was that this dominant bird, the "flockmaster," mates with practically all of the hens, which walk to his station unmolested through the ranks of less privileged males. One such sultan served 21 hens in a morning. Adjacent to the flockmaster is his closest rival, the "subcock," and one step lower in the hierarchy are the "guards," which beat off the lesser gentry but defer to their peers. The subcock and the guards may mate with an occasional hen when the flockmaster is occupied. Thus, natural selection favors the survival of the best stock.

In Europe black grouse similarly divide their dancing grounds into individual territories. First they jump and hoot, an activity highly stimulating to all concerned. Then each male, puffed out and literally shaking, challenges his rival with a bubbling *roo-koo*. With tails widespread and red eye combs swollen, they make short aggressive rushes. Only after the territory has been efficiently defended are they ready to court any female who chooses to walk into it.

In the remnants of natural prairie in North America, prairie chickens still gather each spring on their dancing grounds, where the males strut, inflate orange neck sacs, erect hornlike neck feathers (pinnae) and make hollow booming sounds. This species and a similar prairie grouse, the sharptail, undoubtedly inspired some of the dances of the plains Indians. In their arena the sharptails pivot with rapidly stamping feet, heads down, tails up. When one bird shuffles they all shuffle, when one stops they all stop, in perfect synchronization. The same postures, even the same steps, can be detected in the traditional dances of the Crees.

The ruff, a belligerent Eurasian sandpiper, is unique in that no two males in breeding plumage are exactly alike. Each is adorned with a neck ruff (very suggestive of the frilly ruffs once worn by Dutch burghers) which may be black, white, buff, or rufous-red, and may be plain or barred in endless combinations. The males gather in a small traditional arena to jump, flap their wings and spar; seldom do they tangle in real combat. When the plain-Jane female, the reeve, enters the arena, she seems quite indifferent, whereas the males often

BEGGING BEHAVIOR IN HERRING GULLS

A baby herring gull, just out of the shell, does not immediately associate its parent's bill with feeding. Instinctively, it pecks at the bright red spot near the tip of this long, thin object and receives, in return, a bit of regurgitated fish. So strong is the urge to peck that even a cardboard model (above) will do, if it has a prominent spot. The behaviorist Niko Tinbergen tested the reactions of newly hatched gulls with a variety of dummies, some of them shown below. All worked except the one at bottom left, which had no colored spot and elicited almost no response from the chick. A pencil-thin red rod with white rings on the end for supercontrast proved to be as attractive as the parent's bill.

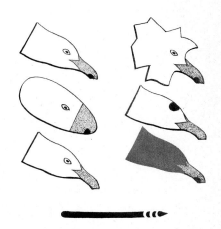

appear to go into shock, crouching motionless while she stands near, possibly making her choice.

Birds, though ritualistic creatures, are undoubtedly capable of a limited amount of learning; witness the jackdaws and ravens trained by Otto Koehler in Germany in the late 1940s that could count up to six or seven, the young nightingales that learn the songs of other birds when isolated from their kind, and the gulls that drop clams on roadways to break the shells. But a bird's world is a narrow one and most of the things it does are mechanistic. A certain set number of situations are met with stereotyped responses. Occasionally, however, a bird meets a situation that is not in its book. What does it do then? Usually something that is singularly inappropriate, such as picking up a stick, making as if to preen itself or bursting into song. This has been called "displacement activity." It finds its human analogy in such nervous actions as key twirling, scratching an ear, coughing uneasily or whistling.

Konrad Lorenz discovered that there was a form of learning that took place very early in a bird's life; to describe it he coined the term "imprinting." He found that if he presented himself to newborn graylag geese hatched in an incubator they immediately identified him as "mother goose." They followed him wherever he went and even swam with him in the Danube, ignoring other geese. Imprinting has now been demonstrated for a number of other birds and attachments have even been recorded between a bird and inanimate objects such as a box or a bottle.

IN contrast to imprinting, wherein newborn birds get impressions that may last throughout their lives, is learning by trial and error. This comes later, when the young bird is finding out about the subtleties of flight, what foods are distasteful or inedible and what situations to avoid.

Such a basic act as feeding nestlings would not seem to require signals, but apparently it does. Young European cuckoos that have pushed their nestmates out are fed by their foster parents simply because they are there, in the right place, and because they gape widely. Meanwhile, the rightful heirs lie outside the nest, dying. They are not fed because they are not in the right place and because, being too weak, they no longer gape for food.

When a bird returns to the nest, young mouths fly open. Actually, a hand held above the nest will release the same response. Equally automatic is the reaction of the parent who, looking down, sees a brightly colored gape, perhaps with a pattern of spots like the throat of a tropical orchid. Down goes the worm. The bird does not try to recall which one was fed last; it reacts to the stimulus of the widest gape. This works well, for the widest is most likely the hungriest.

Many adult gulls have a red or a black spot on the bill. The young bird, by pecking at this spot, stimulates the parent to regurgitate its food. When young birds were experimentally presented with painted pasteboard models they pecked only halfheartedly if the bill lacked such a spot, but if it had one they were most enthusiastic, nor was it necessary that the bill be attached to a head. Even baby gulls hatched under a hen reacted according to form.

All this is part of the birds' innate "language," if we may call it that—a language differing from species to species and which, like all languages, is slowly and constantly evolving. Often misunderstood, sentimentalized or regarded as reflecting an intelligence birds certainly do not have, it remains a fascinating field of study for the ornithologist and behaviorist, an area in which we are learning more and more, not about what birds say, but what they mean—and why.

WITH BASIC ACTIONS ANY BIRD COULD UNDERSTAND, A SONG SPARROW SEEING ITS IMAGE IN A MIRROR ATTACKS THE FANCIED INTRUDER

Language in Action

Song is only one of many ways in which birds express their social instincts, react to their environments and communicate with one another. From the plain aggressiveness shown by this song sparrow to the elaborate rituals of courtship, they can call on a remarkable repertoire of behavior to express themselves in ways often obvious, but often obscure enough to baffle ornithologists.

The Struggle for Living Space

Poets to the contrary, a singing bird is not greeting the spring or proclaiming its joy in life; it is proclaiming territory. However harmonious the sounds it produces, they have an emphatic meaning: a sharp warning to other males of its species to keep out. The fact that its melodies may attract a female ready to nest is a secondary function of that aggressive admonition: it is because she recognizes a male of property, able to support a household, that the female is attracted.

Among different species, however, territories may overlap, and the farm above, seen from a bird's-eye

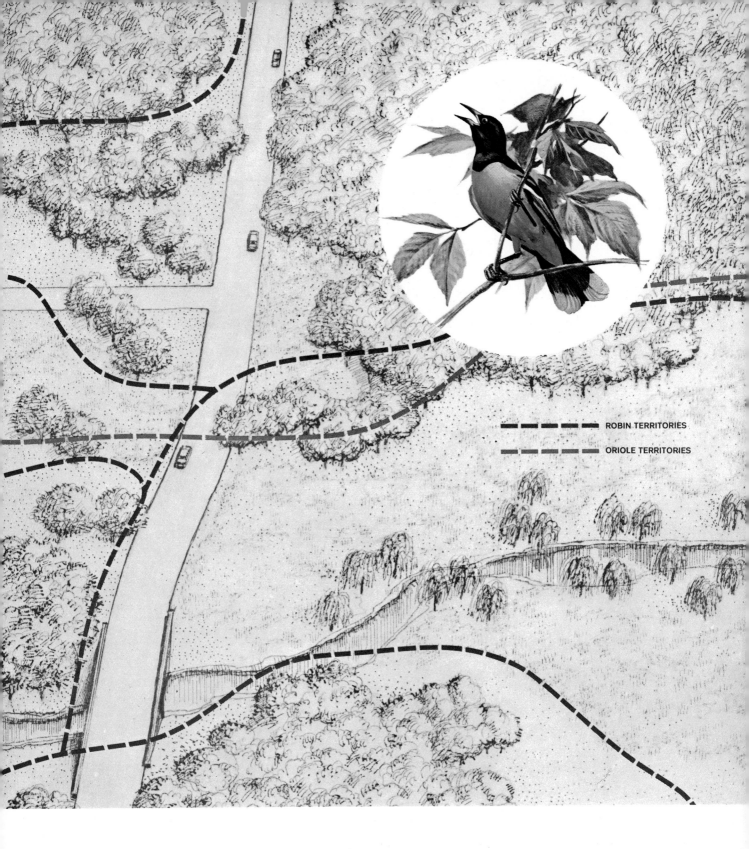

- - - - ROBIN TERRITORIES

- - - - ORIOLE TERRITORIES

view, shows how eight robins (brown lines) and three orioles (green lines) have staked out their living space. Though only two species are shown, this landscape could support as many as 10 or 20 kinds of birds with differing food requirements in peaceful coexistence. The season is mid-May, and two male robins (*lower left*), which have already brought off first broods, are engaged in a border skirmish over territories for their second broods. The Baltimore oriole (*upper right*), an aggressive singer, has just about completed the establishment of its territory, and is ready to set up housekeeping for the first time.

PRESENTING A TWIG, a common egret hands over to its mate the job of guarding their eggs. Male and female alternate at this task. The changing of the guard is always marked by a dancelike ritual, with wings outspread and feathers fluffed, culminating in the presentation of twigs by the bird going off duty. Most egret couples do work together on their nests, but here, with the

nest completed, the contribution is purely ceremonial. The twig itself may very well have come from the nest of the vociferous pair of roseate spoonbills on the left, which share the egrets' breeding territory in the Florida Everglades. Such pilfering sometimes leads to fights, but more likely a guttural squawk is all the protest the comparatively timid spoonbills dare to make.

The Case of the Somersaulting Secretary Bird

The startling gyrations of a secretary bird, shown in these photographs, provide a dramatic example of the problems ornithologists often have to face in interpreting bird behavior. What is this bird doing? When a photographer happened upon it along a roadside in Kenya, East Africa, it was tumbling about all by itself and throwing a small clod of earth into the air. The possibility of a courtship or nesting ritual was ruled out on two counts: there was no other bird of its species nearby, and secretary birds do not dance. Could it have been simply playing? Many birds do, particularly young ones, among which such activity is often important in developing and perfecting reflexes that will be useful to them in later life. More likely, however, in the opinion of three leading East African ornithologists, this secretary bird, which is a snake hunter, was simply dodging a snake that it had pounced upon and missed.

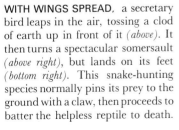

WITH WINGS SPREAD, a secretary bird leaps in the air, tossing a clod of earth up in front of it *(above)*. It then turns a spectacular somersault *(above right)*, but lands on its feet *(bottom right)*. This snake-hunting species normally pins its prey to the ground with a claw, then proceeds to batter the helpless reptile to death.

The Cunning of the Hunted

In a world ruled by fang, beak and claw, birds have one advantage over many of the animals that prey upon them: they can escape by air. Even so, there are occasions when they cannot take wing in the face of danger. The threat may come from another, predatory bird or other creature which preys upon their young or, in the mating season, from an enemy intent upon a meal of eggs.

At such times, birds have to rely on some form of deception to mislead their enemies and protect their young. They may simulate fierceness by aggressive song, by threatening behavior, such as that shown by the sparrow hawk at left, or by trying to look bigger than they are, a trait common among many owls. The least bittern on the right, whose camouflage posture can be very effective when it is surprised in its accustomed surroundings of swamp cattails, tries hard to pretend it is not there at all. The drab appearance of the comparatively vulnerable females and nestlings of most species, even where the males are brightly colored, is another, less dramatic example of camouflage.

The wiles of parent birds in diverting enemies from their eggs and young are numerous and resourceful. Many ground birds whose nests are preyed upon by foxes, weasels and snakes will feign injury in an attempt to draw the predator's attention to themselves. Some birds, including the oystercatcher, will mislead a predator by abandoning their eggs and pretending to brood elsewhere. And the ruffed grouse is always careful to camouflage its nest with a cover of leaves before going off to forage for food.

FLAT ON ITS BACK in a nesting box, a sparrow hawk prepares to defend its eggs with threateningly hooked claws. The female of this species is much larger and fiercer than the male.

DRAGGING ONE WING, a piping plover feigns injury to mislead a predator intent on its eggs. This device is most effective when the spread wing reveals a striking color or pattern.

PUFFING ITS FEATHERS, a short-eared owl attempts to look big and frightening. Feather fluffing to increase apparent body size is practiced by many male birds—usually to bluff each other.

BEAK HIGH AND STRIPED FRONT DISPLAYED, A LEAST BITTERN TRIES TO MERGE INTO ITS REEDY BACKGROUND

GAUDY GAPES like the red-yellow-and-white mouths of these yellowhammer nestlings present obvious targets to parents delivering food. Bright mouth coloring is common among birds that are born helpless.

7

From Egg to Adult

ALL life must replace itself. In our part of the world the annual cycle of the birds, which culminates in their reproduction, has its first vague beginnings when winter gives way to early spring. The foraging flocks are no longer as cooperative in their endless search for food. There is more bickering, more irritable chasing; fragments of song are heard for the first time. The increasing length of the day seems to be affecting the birds' internal rhythm. Great changes are taking place in the gonads, the reproductive glands which are under the control of certain hormones secreted by the anterior pituitary gland. The testes of a male bird may increase in size several hundred times between its quiescent winter period and the peak of the breeding season.

When nesting time approaches, just how does a bird select its territory? After considerable prospecting the male tends to return again and again to the same bush top or the same branch to sing his challenge. He may start with a plot of three or four acres with a number of favorite singing posts, but before he has settled his claim this may be whittled down to half that size by neighboring males who put the pressure on him. As James Fisher describes it: "He plays them at song-tennis over the neutral ground between—ground which rapidly becomes less and less neutral. When one of these neighbors, now become a rival, alights in his area he makes a display flight at it, often singing on the wing; the neighbor retreats into his own area, and if he is followed, the roles are reversed; in such a way the boundaries of the territories are marked out." Years ago Frank Chapman determined the territorial boundaries of birds in his garden by putting up mirrors and noting where the males fought their images.

A singing male is nearly always invincible in his own domain. David Lack once confined a European robin in a cage within its own territory. When a neighboring robin trespassed, the bird in the cage put the intruder to flight simply by the vigor of its song. Conversely, when the caged bird was taken into its neighbor's territory it cowered in terror, prevented by the wire bars from flying away. In a similar experiment Arthur Allen of Cornell University placed a caged song sparrow in the territory of a rival. The confined bird went wild with fear and when the bird outside grabbed its wing tip through the bars it had a heart attack and expired on the floor of the cage.

Territory, as we have seen in Chapter 4, may be simply defined as any area which a bird defends against its own kind. However, perhaps its most functional aspect is that it spaces birds out fairly evenly so that all may be assured of enough food for their growing broods. Typical territories of songbirds in America may range from a half acre or less for some robins up to 22 acres for meadowlarks. James Tanner in his study of the nearly extinct ivory-billed woodpecker in the southeastern U.S. found that a single pair, because of their very specialized habits, required not less than six square miles of virgin swamp timber, whereas the same area could support 36 pairs of pileated woodpeckers or 126 pairs of red-bellied woodpeckers. There is no question that the food resources have a bearing on the sizes and compressibility of territories. S. Charles Kendeigh reported warblers defending territories as small as one tenth of an acre during a spruce budworm outbreak in Canada, when there was more than enough food for all. At the other extreme, a golden eagle, at the apex of the avian pyramid, may dominate a territory of more than 35 square miles.

Colonial birds are usually those with a mobile food supply—gleaners of the air such as swallows or swifts that may travel great distances to find concentrations of flying insects, or sea birds whose luck depends on the vagaries of ocean currents and the schooling of fishes. The critical factor in the affairs of sea birds is a nesting place safe from four-footed predators, preferably an island, and when they find one it becomes the common property of all. They will cooperate in the defense of this communal breeding ground, and birds in a large colony have better nesting success than those in a small one. Within a colony each territory, if it can be called such, is reduced, in effect, to the nest site itself: the distance a bird can strike with its beak while sitting on its eggs. On Isla Raza in the Gulf of California more than 40,000 elegant terns often nest on a single acre of volcanic soil, one for every square foot. Some eggs are scarcely nine inches apart and the birds frequently lock their rapierlike bills with their neighbors while they brood.

In the northern United States, the first robin of spring and the last one to appear may be two months apart. The arrival of red-winged blackbirds may span three months. First to arrive are the stray birds, the vagrants, soon to be followed by high-plumaged males which claim territories they may have held the year before; then by the females, and lastly by the young males, which will fit into the population mosaic as vacancies permit.

If a territory is vacant, it is quickly filled by such an unemployed male. We have already cited the replacement of birds in a Maine spruce forest after the resident birds were shot off. In a similarly ruthless but enlightening experiment in New Jersey some years ago, a male indigo bunting was collected after it had mated. By next morning the female had another mate. Nine times in about as many days the males were removed and each time the female succeeded in quickly acquiring another partner.

The female, on first arriving in a territory, is threatened by the male, just as the same male would threaten another male. But there is a difference; she neither fights nor does she fly away. By various subtle means she takes the aggressive wind out of the male's sails and his attitude switches to appeasement. She may not be fully conscious of the territory at first. She may wander away, only to be lured back by the irresistible song. There are sexual pursuits; the male desires copulation but she may not be ready. Or there may be special displays and perhaps courtship feeding. At any rate, the preliminaries are very stimulating and within a matter of days the female reaches the oestrus, or comes into heat; she is in harmony with the male and is receptive to copulation.

One or both of this pair, now on the threshold of mating, may have pipped the egg only the year before. Most songbirds and ducks mate for the first time when they are scarcely 12 months old. Herring gulls, however, take at least three years to reach full maturity while eagles may take four or five. Sea birds like albatrosses, as noted, take longest of all: they do not mate before they are skilled enough at their trade to assume the responsibility of raising a chick.

The creation of the nest is inextricably tied in with courtship and sexual fulfillment. There is nothing in the fossil record to suggest how such a complicated habit evolved, but some ethologists believe it may have started quite simply—perhaps from the movements of the birds during sexual excitement. A female tern, for example, pivots on her breast to face the male who is circling about her with drooping wings, and eventually a saucerlike "scrape" is formed in the sand. Some terns lay their eggs in this depression without further embellishment; others add pebbles or sticks. The more complex nests of many other birds may have had just such simple origins.

Most nest building is done the natural way, while sitting. At first the bird may squat in a clump of grass, punching or molding it with its breast, or it may try to fit its body into a likely crotch in a shrub or tree. A few twigs or straws may be pushed into place. If they do not stick the bird may try another site. Eventually, by tucking, poking, pushing and molding, the cup takes shape.

No two species build identical nests. An expert observer does not always have to see the eggs to know the maker of the nest; the materials, size, structure and location are clues to his practiced eye. Nests vary from none at all, not even a scrape, as in the case of nightjars and other whippoorwill-like birds which lay their well-camouflaged eggs on the bare ground, to the exquisitely woven purses of orioles and troupials and the complicated basketry of the weavers.

Just which birds make the smallest nests and which the largest is a matter of dispute. Some hummingbirds build nests scarcely an inch in diameter, but just as small is the tiny saucer of bark, down and dried glue in which the crested tree swift fits its single egg. A famous bald eagle nest at Vermilion, Ohio, measured eight and a half feet in diameter, 12 feet in depth and weighed about two tons. Another supernest built by a pair of eagles near St. Petersburg, Florida, had a diameter of nine and a half feet and a depth of 20.

A KNOTTY PROBLEM
IN NEST CONSTRUCTION

Many of the sparrowlike weaverbirds of Africa are among the world's best nest builders. Their technique is based on the ability to hold down a grass strand with the foot (above) while wrapping, knotting or weaving the other end with the beak. The nest starts with the suspension of a woven ring of grass from a branch or leaf. The bird then stands in this ring and works in other long strands of grass all around until it is enclosed in a loose hollow ball slightly larger than itself. As many as 300 grass strands have been used in a nest. An inner partition keeps eggs from falling from the entrance at the bottom.

Even greater in diameter than the eyries of eagles are the huge mounds of the megapodes, strange Australasian fowl that do not use their body heat to incubate their eggs. Instead, they pile up great heaps of debris which serve as incubators; the warmth of the fermenting compost does the work. In one species, the scrub fowl, a mound 20 feet high and 50 feet wide has been reported.

The tiny cobwebs-and-floss cup of the hummer and the gross untidy heap of the megapode are but two extremes in an extraordinary variety of avian architecture. Woodpeckers excavate their nurseries. These chambers, which often double as off-season sleeping quarters, are not lined; the eggs are laid on a bed of scattered chips. But the birds that make use of these holes when they are abandoned—titmice, wrens, flycatchers, swallows, bluebirds and others—build substantial nests inside.

The open-topped bowl typical of many land birds may be deep and felted like that of a goldfinch, shallow and twiggy like a dove's, or firmly woven of grass and hair as is a warbler's wont. The American robin and European song thrush reinforce their nests with a mortar of mud, and vireos and the chaffinch bind theirs together with cobwebs. Nests may be anywhere from the ground to 100 feet or more up in the tallest trees, although only a small percentage are higher than 20 feet and the majority are within six or eight feet of the ground. The nests of most small birds are built in a week or less. A song sparrow in a hurry might finish a nest, and a good one too, in as little as three days, or it may dawdle along for nearly two weeks; its pace possibly reflects the stage of its glandular cycle.

Male wrens, overflowing with energy, build dummy nests or cock nests. In a reed bed where many globular nests of long-billed marsh wrens are fastened to the cattails, only one in half a dozen may hold eggs or young.

The mythical halcyon, the kingfisher, was rumored to lay its eggs on the quiet waters of the sea, hence the lovely term "halcyon days." Actually, kingfishers nest in tunnels they dig in riverbanks—or occasionally in the mounds of termites. Their nest burrows may extend for six or seven feet, but those of bee eaters and some other earth excavators may be even longer.

No birds, of course, lay their eggs in the water, but grebes come close to it, laying theirs on small rafts of debris or decaying vegetation drifting about in the marsh. When the bird slips into the water it deftly pulls some of the vegetation over the eggs. This instinctive action serves two purposes: the eggs are concealed and, as a thermometer would reveal, their temperature is regulated. Ducks accomplish the same thing by wrapping their eggs in a quilt of down from their own breasts.

Mud is a useful medium for the construction of nests. Flamingos make conical mounds which may be nearly two feet high, building them up pellet by pellet. Cliff swallows and house martins fasten their mud jugs under ledges, bridges and eaves. The rufous ovenbird, the national bird of Argentina, mixes a mortar of sand and cow dung to construct a nine-pound ball with a door on one side and an inner spiral threshold. The crossbar of nearly every telephone pole along the roadside supports one of these rock-hard ovens of *el hornero*, "the baker."

Among the most skilled bird artisans are those which suspend their nests. The vireos of North America weave firm little baskets hung from the V-forks of lateral twigs. The nests of orioles, swinging from the tip-ends of slender branches, are deeper and more purselike. Their colonial relatives, the oropendolas of the American tropics, knit "socks" three feet long, taking a month to do the job.

Twenty or 30 such long bags may dangle from the perimeter of a single ceiba tree. The ultimate in simplicity of suspension is achieved by the green broadbill of Malaya, which hangs its intricately woven nest over a woodland pool by means of a single long woven string.

In building such hanging nests, the attachment of the first few strands of plant fiber presents a problem in engineering. The Australian rock warbler solves this by gluing its frail pouch to the roof of a cave by means of sticky spider webs. The weaverbirds of Africa and southern Asia actually tie knots. Some weavers build very sophisticated hanging nests which are entered through a vertical sleeve projecting several inches below the globular nesting chamber, which itself has a little guard rail to prevent the eggs from falling through. Whether ingenuity or accident originally played a part in these designs we cannot know, but it is axiomatic that whenever a device favored survival it was likely to be preserved. Certainly in the tropics, where agile monkeys are a menace, the hanging nest is one answer to survival—and so is the frequent habit of building close to the nests of hornets and other stinging or biting insects, or even right inside, as some birds do, particularly in the nests of termites.

F EW birds in the world construct weirder nests than the swifts. Most of the 76 species of swifts employ their saliva, which hardens to the consistency of rock. The chimney swift of North America, which used to build in hollow trees, now glues its bracket of sticks on the inner wall of man-made stacks. The swallow-tailed swifts of tropical America use saliva and feathers to build feltlike tubes up to two feet long which hang beneath rocky shelves. But the most improbable device of all is that of the palm swift of the Old World tropics, which glues its two eggs *upright* on a feltlike pad stuck onto a drooping palm leaf. Even when the leaf sways, flaps or turns upside down, the eggs stick, and so does the brooding bird.

The little cave swiftlets of the Indo-Australasian region use more saliva than other swifts and two kinds build their little bracketlike saucers entirely of this agglutinate material. These are the famous birds' nests of Oriental commerce from which such delicious soup is made. Tremendous numbers of swiftlets colonize some of the limestone caverns along the coast of Indochina, and here men reap their odd harvest with long poles, knocking down fresh nests which have taken more than a month to build.

The emperor penguin, the largest of the penguin family, needs no nest at all. Its single youngster is brought forth in the dead of the antarctic winter when the temperatures drop to 40° F. below zero. The female lays her egg in May just as the long antarctic night is setting in and the male immediately takes over. He places the egg on top of his feet where the warm skin and feathers of the belly sag to form a protective mantle. Bracing himself against the coldest winds on earth, which may reach 100 miles an hour, and gaining some warmth from his fellows who crowd cheek to jowl on the ice, this brooding father patiently nurtures the germ of life for more than two months until the chick hatches. He will have lost 25 pounds, a third of his weight, before the well-fed female slides in at last to relieve him and feed the chick.

Colonies such as those of herons or terns, which are like crowded cities with their individual homes, are not the only examples of how birds nest cooperatively. The emperor penguins in their milling pod on the ice are plainly cooperating. The sociable weaver of South Africa builds a regular apartment house so large that at a distance it might be mistaken for a native hut. As many as 100 pairs

AN OVEN OF CLAY FOR THE 'BAKER'S' EGGS

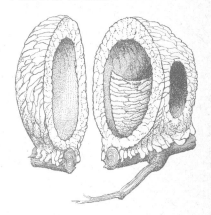

The rufous ovenbird of South America, nicknamed the "baker," builds a hollow ball for a nest from a mortar of sand and cow dung so strong that a thrown rock will not crack it. The nest above is cut open to reveal how the eggs are safeguarded by a semipartition between the entrance vestibule (right) and the nest chamber (left).

or more may build what appears to be a haystack 12 or 15 feet in diameter in the branches of an isolated tree on the veldt. First to be built is the roof, and under it each bird tucks its own nesting chamber. In Argentina the monk parakeet builds similar collective dwellings of sticks with as many as a score of screeching families occupying flats in the main building.

Must birds learn how to build nests or do they know by instinct? We do not know to what extent the young bird's memory of its natal environs is important, but there is one case on record in which four generations of captive weaverbirds had no chance to build nests—but the fifth generation built them quite competently when they were given nest-building materials.

The laying of the eggs is synchronized with the building of the nest and may start the day after the last stick or straw has been pushed into place. Some birds take a breather for several days before beginning to lay. In most of the perching birds the usual rate is one egg a day, laid in the early morning, but the parasitic European cuckoo steals a march on its neighbors by sneaking in during the afternoon, to lay its own egg in another bird's nest. We tend to think of this as low cunning on the cuckoo's part, but more likely it is a result of natural selection: cuckoos have profited by deviating from the morning routine.

Not all birds lay on a 24-hour schedule. Many have a somewhat longer interval; quite a few hawks, owls and gulls, for instance, lay on alternate days. Some eagles and condors space their eggs five days apart, while the mallee fowl has an interval of five to nine days (exceptionally, 16) and may take as long as four months to complete its quota. It can afford to take its time, since it is one of the megapodes, or mound birds, and is therefore not saddled with the tedium of incubation.

The number of eggs a bird lays might be taken as an index to its life expectancy. By inference, hummingbirds, laying only two eggs, have fewer hazards or greater longevity than wrens which rear two broods of six or seven in a single summer. An albatross or a petrel lays but a single egg and if it is lost will not lay another that year. On the other hand, a pheasant or a duck may lay 12 or even 15 in a single clutch. These game birds have always led a precarious existence and it must not be concluded that their large broods are a direct result of gunning pressure—man is only one of many animals which prey on them and their eggs. But given half a chance they recover quickly from disaster; their reproductive potential is high.

THE tiniest eggs are those of hummingbirds, pea-sized, almost always two and always white. Among living birds the largest, as one would expect, are laid by the ostrich. Five to seven inches long and with very thick shells, they take 40 minutes to hard boil.

Tiny birds with prolific tendencies, such as blue tits, long-tailed tits, goldcrests and kinglets, may produce a single clutch that exceeds their own body weight. So may some ducks. A ruddy duck, which lays the largest eggs of any duck for its size, may weigh scarcely more than a pound, whereas its average clutch of nine eggs tips the scales at nearly two pounds and a very large clutch of 14 or 15 would exceed three pounds.

Not all eggs are "egg-shaped." The eggs of owls and toucans are nearly spherical. Those of the murres and other auks are pear-shaped, a decided advantage on the narrow rock shelves where they are laid, for they pivot without rolling off. The other seafowl that share the cliffs—the gulls, cormorants and gannets—must build nests to keep their eggs in place.

Archaeopteryx and all the other dawn birds must have laid unmarked whitish eggs as reptiles do today. Many birds still lay immaculate white eggs, particularly those that nest in dark holes where camouflage would be superfluous—the kingfishers, woodpeckers, swifts, parrots, owls, bee eaters and practically all of the tropical hole nesters.

Most eggs laid in open nests are speckled, spotted, blotched or lined; some are very effectively camouflaged. Since the pigment which effects the coloration is deposited on the shell during its passage through the oviduct, much variation results and no two eggs are marked precisely alike. The pigment on the heavily blotched egg of a ptarmigan, almost blood-red when freshly laid, soon oxidizes until it becomes almost black. It has been suggested that these pigments, which are related to those of the blood and the bile, are merely by-products with no more usefulness or significance than the colors that appear on autumn leaves. True or not, what beautiful by-products!

Do birds recognize their own eggs? That is debatable. In a colony of terns the egg patterns vary from tiny specks to large blotches and, nesting as they do often only a beak's thrust from each other, it would seem that egg recognition would be important to terns. However, experiments show that even in such crowded circumstances it is the site that is the magnet. A tern will brood even a flash bulb if it is in the right place. If its own egg (or any egg) is placed several inches in front of the empty nest it will retrieve it, rolling it back into the scrape, but at a greater distance the same egg will be ignored. However, on Midway Island, when a sooty tern (which lays only one egg) was given a choice of two eggs, it usually retrieved its own, so apparently there is a measure of recognition.

Other colonial birds react in much the same way. A herring gull will brood brightly painted wooden eggs and night herons will accept wooden blocks with uncomfortable corners even though they can see their own eggs two or three feet away.

Songbirds, even those that nest on the ground, will not retrieve their eggs should they roll outside the rim. Some species will also refuse to brood the eggs of cowbirds, seeming to recognize that they are unlike the rest. Most small birds, however, readily accept the eggs of these parasites; they may even be stimulated by their large size.

Nearly 80 species of birds belonging to several families are completely parasitic at nesting time, laying their eggs in nests not their own and leaving the care of their young to their hosts. A number of other species are partially parasitic, usually building their own nests and caring for their own young but sometimes laying in other nests. The greatest number of these "nonobligate" parasites are found among the ducks. More than 20 species lay, at least occasionally, in the nests of their neighbors, and one, the redhead of North America, does so more often than not. Milton Weller records that 13 different female redheads laid eggs in the same nest and as many as 87 eggs have been found in a single "dump" nest. Only one duck, the black-headed duck of South America, is believed to be completely parasitic, for no nest has ever been recorded. Its eggs have been found not only in the reedy baskets of other ducks but also in the nests of gulls, glossy ibises and even chimangos, small birds of prey!

The honey guides, essentially African, parasitize their relatives, the barbets. To insure its survival the bill of the young honey guide at birth is equipped with a pair of hooks, as sharp as needles, with which it gives a fatal nip to its nest-mates. A few days later, the hooks, no longer needed, fall off.

A PATERNAL THERMOSTAT

MALLEE FOWL

The mallee fowl uses the heat of fermenting vegetable matter to help incubate its eggs. They are deposited in a huge pile of decaying leaves and trash collected by the male bird and covered by a layer of sand. Proper temperature is maintained by constant adjustment of the sand covering. This task is practically the lifetime career of the mallee male (shown below testing the temperature with his beak). The female is permitted to approach the mound only to lay an egg, which she does about once a week for several months. As each chick hatches, it struggles unaided up through the sand to face life on its own. Neither parent seems even to recognize its offspring.

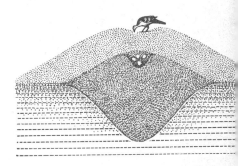

MALLEE NEST

The most famous of all parasitic birds is the cuckoo of Eurasia and Africa. Over 300 species of birds are parasitized by this master nestfinder. To make room for itself in a small nest the young cuckoo squirms and shoves until its nestmates or the unhatched eggs are heaved overboard. The oölogists Edgar Chance and Stuart Baker assert that a cuckoo tends to lay its eggs in nests like the one in which it was raised and the eggs themselves are surprisingly similar to those of their hosts, even as to color. Perhaps imprinted with the nest of its foster parent, the bird carries this impression through life. One strain of cuckoos may lay only in the nests of meadow pipits while another may specialize in willow warblers. Critics point out that the Chance and Baker theory may prove to be true but that they failed to color-mark the adult cuckoos to make sure of their identity.

Whereas half the Old World cuckoos are parasitic, the New World cuckoos, with only four exceptions, are not. However, both the yellow-billed and the black-billed cuckoo of America will occasionally lay in other nests. It is among some of these occasional or partial parasites that we find hints about the intriguing question of how the parasitic habit evolved.

In the New World the cowbirds are the principal parasitic group. Each young cowbird is raised at the expense of one or two young of its host, a circumstance that causes biologically untutored "bird lovers" to smash every cowbird's egg they find. Actually, the survival percentages of cowbirds are no greater than those of their host species and to remove all the cowbird's eggs does not increase the numbers of redstarts, song sparrows or red-eyed vireos one bit.

Some birds are "determinate" layers. A typical sandpiper or plover lays four eggs, no more, and if one is taken it does not make up the loss; it always lays four, then stops. "Indeterminate" layers will keep on if their eggs are taken. They apparently must feel the proper number in the nest before they stop. A flicker whose egg was removed each day laid 71 eggs in 73 days; a European wryneck laid 62 eggs in 62 days. Domestic fowl fall into this category, the record for a chicken being 361 eggs in a year. A duck did even better, laying 363 eggs in 365 days.

Broodiness is thus triggered in one of these two ways: by the physiological process of having laid the right number of eggs or by the tactile sensation of sitting on the right number. Most perching birds and precocial birds (ducks, geese, grouse, etc.) do not start incubation until the clutch is about complete. This gives all the young, which hatch fairly close together, an equal start in

ALTRICIAL BIRDS–HELPLESS AT BIRTH

The young of most birds are blind, naked and utterly helpless at birth. They emerge from the egg in a relatively undeveloped condition and require constant parental care and feeding until they gain strength, grow feathers and are able to leave the nest. Birds of this type are called altricial. Reflecting the short time that they spend in the egg, their eggs tend to be small. The meadowlark, a typical altricial bird, hatches in about two weeks and leaves the nest 10 to 12 days later.

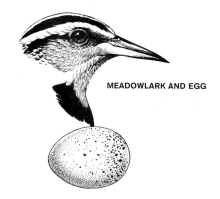

MEADOWLARK AND EGG

DAY-OLD CHICK

life. Hawks, owls, parrots, herons, storks and a number of other large birds, however, incubate from the day the first egg is laid, with the result that the youngsters hatch at intervals. There is often such a difference in sizes in barn owls that big brother may kill and eat little brother when the latter hatches.

Although the germ of life, the embryo, begins to develop even before the egg leaves the warmth of the bird's body, its growth is arrested temporarily when the egg is laid, to be resumed when the bird starts the long—11 to 80 days—chore of incubation. The embryo grows rapidly, absorbing the whites and most of the yolk. A day or two before hatching it actually starts breathing, taking its oxygen from the air chamber and through the porous shell. Meanwhile the shell is getting weaker, for much of its lime has been absorbed by the bones of the growing skeleton.

MERELY sitting on the eggs does not insure their incubation. Feathers are insulation; to transmit heat to the eggs birds develop "brood spots," bare patches on the underbody. The down falls out, the fat disappears and a concentration of blood vessels raises the temperature of the skin. Settling on the eggs, the bird parts its abdominal feathers and shimmies its body so that these spots come into comfortable contact with the eggs. In general these patches, numbering from one to three in different species, are present only in the sex that broods; if both sexes share the labor, both have them. But not all birds have this thermostatic incubation aid. Ducks do not, but they compensate by pulling out the down themselves and adding it to the nest. Gannets do not have them either; they place a big webbed foot on the single egg, like a warming pad.

Periodically, perhaps as often as a dozen times an hour, the bird turns the eggs or adjusts them to the brood patch. However, they need not be covered constantly. Although the average temperature of an egg may be in the low 90s, it is addled more readily by exposure to the hot sun than by cooling. Herons, terns, sandpipers and other birds that spell each other (often with an ostentatious change-over ceremony) may brood nearly 100 per cent of the time. But in most perching birds, where the female alone is responsible, she may spend 15 to 30 minutes at a time on the eggs and then take a break of anywhere from six to 10 minutes for feeding.

Incubation may take as little as 11 days in some perching birds, but as long as 80 days in kiwis and large albatrosses. There is one record of a mallee fowl's egg that took 90 days (instead of the average 62).

The mallee fowl, incidentally, takes extraordinary care of its incubator nest. The male spends more than five hours a day regulating the temperature of the

DAY-OLD CHICK

KILLDEER AND EGG

PRECOCIAL BIRDS– ACTIVE AT BIRTH

Certain birds, like the killdeer, are able to fend for themselves almost immediately on hatching. They are known as precocial. Although the killdeer is about the same size as the meadowlark, its egg is considerably larger, reflecting the longer time (24 to 28 days) its chick will remain inside before hatching and also the greater amount of yolk needed to feed this larger chick. Some precocial chicks can run and feed themselves in an hour, others are unable to do so for as much as two days.

145

nest-mound, testing it with its beak or tongue. By opening up the mound or piling on more sand it keeps the egg chamber at an even 92° F. This cannot be called a laborsaving device, for the male spends 11 months a year on maintenance work. Its relative, the maleo of Celebes, lays its eggs in the warm black volcanic sands of beaches and even near hot springs or steaming fissures on the sides of volcanoes.

The family relationship of the mallee fowl is almost reptilian; the chick never knows either parent. As soon as it burrows out of the mound, which may take from 2 to 15 hours, it is on its own and fully able to fly. No female has ever been seen with a brood. The biographer of this strange bird, H. J. Frith, points out that if the female were to collect her year's progeny she would ultimately have a brood of up to 30 chicks, varying in age from a few days to several months.

To pip the shell the unborn bird is equipped with an "egg tooth," a small horny nubbin on the tip of the upper mandible with which it chips away at its prison. A sign of the bird's reptile ancestry, this temporary growth disappears soon after birth, just as it does on the snakes and lizards that also have it. The actual hatching process may take from several hours to a day or more. As much as two days before hatching, the chick may be heard peeping faintly within the shell and it is then, according to Tinbergen, that the parent first regards the fetus as a chick, not an egg.

When the struggling young bird finally kicks itself free, the parent may eat the empty shell or remove it, flying some distance with it if the young are not the sort that leave the nest right away. Grouse, quail and ducks, whose chicks can walk when they are hatched, usually abandon the collection of castoff shells where they are.

THE young of birds fall into two main categories. Those which are helpless, born blind, naked and feeble, with little talent at first except to open their mouths and to defecate, are called *altricial*. The helpless young of some sea birds, herons, hawks, and owls are also included under this term even though they may start life with a covering of down. *Precocial* chicks are fully clothed, bright-eyed and able to run after their parents and peck at things as soon as the down dries. The rule of thumb is that precocial birds lay larger eggs than altricial birds of similar size.

The precocial bird, born alert, has a relatively long infancy; the altricial bird, often eating its own weight in a day, soon outstrips it. A young songbird, born naked and helpless, eats and grows at a furious rate. A young European cuckoo, two grams at birth, weighs 50 times as much three weeks later. During this period of intensive bodybuilding, the diet of young birds runs heavily to insects, even though it may shift later to seeds or fruit.

If the young may be called growth machines, the parents are tireless feeding automatons, constantly stoking the furnace. A pair of phoebes was reported to make 845 trips to the nest in a day, a pair of great tits 900. An eagle, on the other hand, may make only two or three daily trips, but the prey it brings to its hungry young is large.

Whether the fledged bird is a warbler that leaves the nest in nine days and is fed for two weeks longer or an albatross that makes its first flight to sea at the age of six months, it is at last on its own and the next few months will prove whether it will survive. Mortality is greatest in the first year. When the next breeding season rolls around, there should, in theory, be just about the same number of pairs on territory as there were the year before.

TAKING ITS TURN FORAGING, A MALE RED-NECKED GREBE RETURNS TO THE FAMILY'S FLOATING HOME WITH A WATER INSECT FOR ITS YOUNG

The Family Life of Birds

Each spring, as the warmth and light of lengthening days wakes the landscape, birds begin their annual cycle of courtship, repro- duction, nest-building, incubation and brooding their young. Some birds carry out only a few of these functions in the course of brief liaisons. Others form close-knit, enduring families or even large communities. But either way, new life for the future is insured.

A MALE WANDERING ALBATROSS STARTS COURTSHIP BY FLAPPING ITS WINGS (LEFT). AFTER SOME NIBBLING, IT ATTRACTS ANOTHER FEMALE.

The Ritual of Courtship

Birds, like people, when courting put their best foot forward, showing off their particular skills or attributes to the greatest possible advantage. Thus, versatile fliers like the skylark or the woodcock engage in impressive courtship flights, while species with highly spectacular markings, like pheasants and peacocks, resort to elaborate plumage display to attract prospective partners. Among many sparrows and other dull-coated species, however, the sexes look pretty much alike, so that these birds must rely on song rather than sight to find a mate. Still other birds have evolved long and intricate rites which strengthen the bond for the many months the pair will spend together caring for the eggs and young. Examples of birds with remarkable dances are the cranes, the tree ducks and the nibbling, hopping, yowling albatrosses which are seen prancing across these pages.

HUGE WING SPAN of a wandering albatross, like this one photographed on an antarctic island, may measure almost 11 feet.

SOON THE INTRUDER IS DRIVEN AWAY AND THE PAIR REACHES A CLIMAX (BELOW) AS BOTH BIRDS STRETCH THEIR WINGS AND SHRIEK LOUDLY.

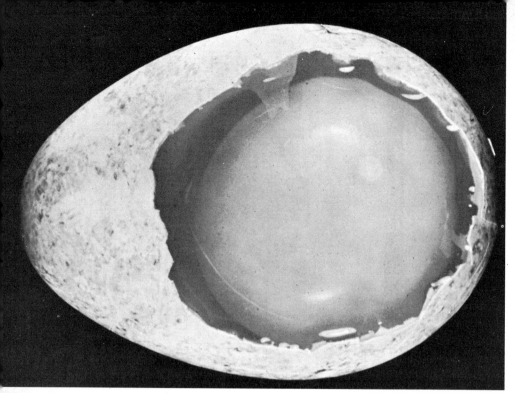

A NEWLY LAID EGG

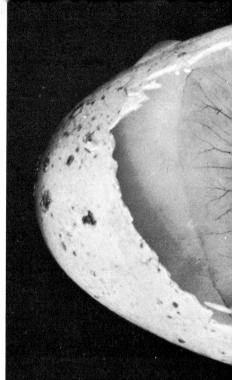

5 DAYS OLD

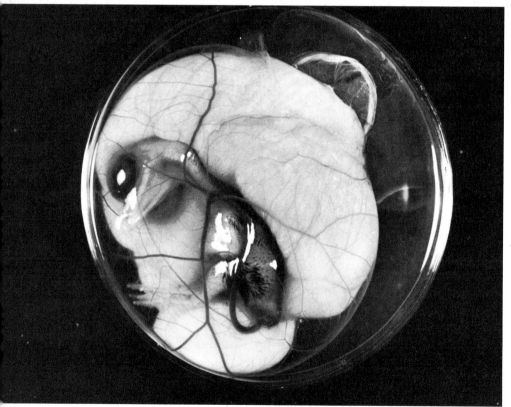

15 DAYS OLD

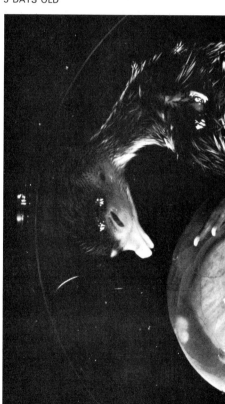

23 DAYS OLD

Stages in the Development of the Avian Egg

Although the time it takes an egg to hatch varies considerably among species, the growth process inside the shell is the same for all birds and is illustrated in these photographs of a turkey embryo in different stages of its development. The newly laid egg shows little more than a huge yolk which will

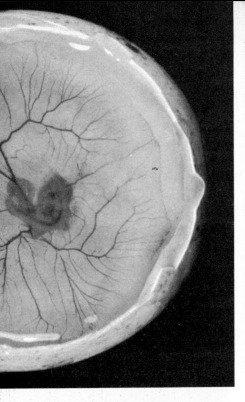

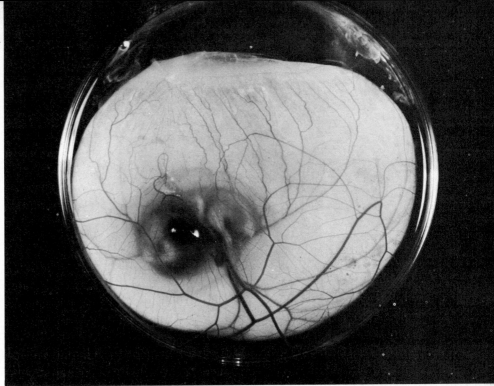

12 DAYS OLD

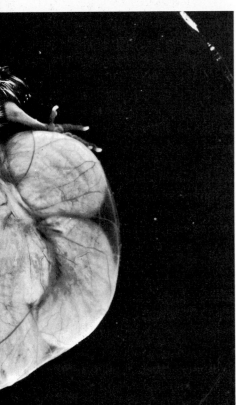

29 DAYS OLD

nourish the growing chick. Five days later, the embryo's outlines are already visible and a network of blood vessels that absorb sustenance from the yolk has radiated across its surface. By the 12th day, except for a single connective stalk the embryo is completely separated from the shrinking yolk. At 15 days various organs can be clearly discerned, particularly the eyes. At 23 days the bird is fully formed and begins to absorb the remaining yolk into its abdomen. Finally, about four weeks after the egg was laid, the living bird accepts its first challenge and beaks its way into the world outside.

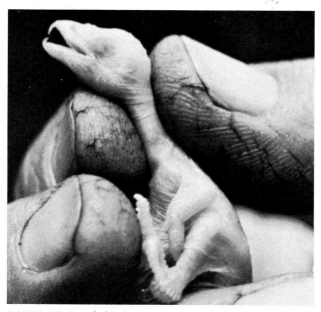
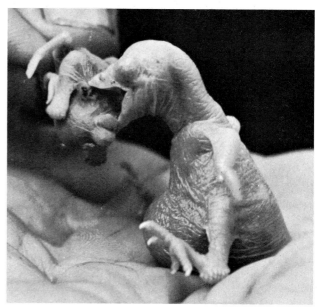

A NEED TO BITE helps insure the survival of a baby African honey guide. Immediately on hatching, it instinctively uses the sharp hooks on its bill to nip and kill the rightful occupants of the nest, most often young barbets. Their work done, the hooks drop off. Honey guides, like most parasites, are laid only one to a nest. If more were laid, they would begin killing each other off.

Deadly Nestmates

Not all birds are good homemakers. Some species, particularly the cowbirds and cuckoos, depend on others to do this work for them. The bay-winged cowbird, for example, often waits for another bird to build a nest, then appropriates it. But as soon as this is done, its cousin, the screaming cowbird, may sneak in and lay an egg in the bay-wing's stolen nest. The African widow bird, also a busy parasite, mates with a succession of females, each of which may then lay her eggs in different waxbill nests.

The interloper's egg is often the first to hatch. Being older and usually bigger than other nestlings, the parasite can get rid of them by pushing them about, stepping on them and starving them. The adult birds do not discriminate between the babies they feed; they simply stuff food into the biggest and nearest mouth. A few parasites eliminate nestmates directly, as is illustrated above and below.

AN IMPULSE TO SHOVE impels a blind European cuckoo—which hatches earlier than its nestmates—to work the eggs of a tree pipit out of the nest, leaving only itself to be raised by the foster parents. The pushing reflex, which lasts some four days, is set off when a sensitive area on the bird's back comes into contact with solid objects like eggs, chicks, and even marbles.

AN INSTINCT TO FEED whatever lies in its nest has impelled this dunnock (or "hedge sparrow") to go on dropping insects in a cuckoo's mouth after the latter has outgrown its host and left the nest. Hosts even perch on adopted chicks' backs to do the job. Sparrows, warblers and other small parasitized birds will continue to cater to imposters several times their own size.

GREAT HORNED OWL
Bubo virginianus

BLACK SKIMMER
Rynchops nigra

BALTIMORE ORIOLE
Icterus galbula

COMMON SNIPE
Capella gallinago

COMMON MURRE
Uria aalge

AMERICAN COOT
Fulica americana

SCRUB FOWL
Megapodius freycinet

SNOWY EGRET
Leucophoyx thula

EMU
Dromiceius novaehollandiae

CARDINAL
Richmondena cardinalis

GUIRA CUCKOO
Guira guira

ROBIN
urdus migratorius

NORTH ISLAND KIWI
Apteryx australis

JAÇANA
Jacana spinosa

BROAD-BILLED HUMMINGBIRD
Cynanthus latirostris

CRESTED TINAMOU
Eudromia elegans

NEW GUINEA MANUCODE
(BIRD OF PARADISE)
Manucodia ater

COMMON CROW
Corvus brachyrhynchos

WHITE PELICAN
Pelecanus erythrorhynchos

The Diversity of Eggs

The largest bird egg known is that of the extinct elephant bird, shown here in white outline behind some representative eggs of living birds, all painted in actual size. This huge egg held over two gallons —30,000 times as much as the smallest hummingbird's egg; its shell was also 75 times as thick.

Generally speaking, egg size is related to that of the bird that lays it, but there are some notable exceptions. The kiwi, for example, is less than half the size of the white pelican, but its egg is several times

as large. It is, in fact, the largest in proportion to its parent's size of any egg. This also explains its long shape; if it were rounder, the female could not lay it. Eggs laid on sea ledges, like the murre's, are often sharply tapered. If they roll, they roll in tight circles and do not fall off.

Differences in color seem to mean little, except that speckles camouflage eggs laid on the ground. White eggs often belong to birds that nest in holes or burrows—their conspicuousness is no problem.

155

HALF-BUILT HANG NEST of a male baya weaver will soon be completed now that the tiny tropical architect has lured a shopping female into sharing it. This type of nest provides excellent protection against marauding monkeys and tree snakes of the Asian jungles.

SEWN HOME of the redheaded tailorbird i actually stitched together with plant fibers The bird punches holes along the edges o

A PRIMITIVE SCRAPE in coarse sand surrounded by a few pebbles and vegetation serves the Arctic tern as a nest. The bird spends most of its life traveling and uses but little time to build.

A Diversity of Architecture

There are almost as many ways to build nests and as many materials from which to construct them as there are species to build them. Mud, wood chips, feathers, stones, twigs and grass are among the popular substances used to form homes that may be as crude as the vague depression made in the grass by the red-throated diver, or as elaborate as the snug, two-chambered sand and dung house of the rufous ovenbird. Saliva is often used by swifts to cement materials together. Many species are attracted by bright decorative objects like pins, papers, wires, golf balls and bottles, which they incorporate into nest construction. In fact, one observer reported that

large green leaves with its bill and threads fibers through the holes, expertly drawing the leaves into a cup to hold its dangling nest.

GRASS HOUSE of the reed-dwelling yellow-eyed babbler is bound with silver-gray strands of spider cobwebs. These strong filaments also anchor the structure firmly between stems. The whole nest is built close to the ground and concealed by the foliage.

a pair of Bombay crows formed a nest with some $70 worth of gold eyeglass frames which they had stolen from an open shopwindow.

Sometimes male and female will work together to build a home, alternately gathering material and shaping the nest. Such cooperation is notable among kingfishers, swallows and woodpeckers. Just as often, one or the other sex will take on the whole job. But whether the final product is simple, sloppy, neat or as intricate as the nests seen above, it usually provides at least two basic amenities: safety from predators and close proximity to a source of food, and often shelter against extreme weather.

FLIMSY STRUCTURE of the mourning dove is built both by the male, which gathers the material, and the female, which does the actual building. This one in a cactus is safe from predators.

157

EXTRACTING PIGEON'S MILK, a secretion chemically similar to rabbit's milk, a white-faced quail dove sucks at the inner side of its parent's crop. Both sexes manufacture the fluid.

Predigested Meals

The majority of perching birds feed their young by the familiar method of placing their insect-laden beaks directly in the hatchling's mouth. But some orders, particularly the big sea birds, have developed more complex feeding techniques. These birds swallow their food where they catch it, semidigest it and regurgitate the gruel back at the nest. This not only lets the bird carry more food per trip, but it also helps the youngster to digest it, since the parent regurgitates digestive juices along with the marine creatures it has swallowed.

The simplest form of this kind of feeding is found among gulls and storks. They throw up the food in front of the nestlings, which quickly devour it. Adult albatrosses and spoonbills go a step further; they grab hold of the hatchling's beak crosswise in their bills and shovel the food down with their tongues.

MINING A MEAL from deep within its parent's gullet, this brown pelican chick and its nestmate will each consume 150 pounds of regurgitated food before they are old enough to fly.

159

A JUICY MASS OF LARVAE is rammed into an avid chick's beak by a black-throated green warbler. This warbler is one of the many small species that make 200 or more food sorties each day to quell the fierce appetites of their dependents. The male warbler assumes much of the responsibility during the feeding period, making three times as many trips as the female.

A FECAL SAC is removed from its nest by a female lyrebird (*above*) and added to previously discarded sacs in a nearby stream (*below*). These sacs of thin membrane, formed in the intestines of young birds, make neat packages for disposal of body wastes. They are important to the survival of low-nesting species, for without them the droppings might lure predators.

Parental Care

Along with providing food, many adult birds take extensive care of their young, brooding them, enticing them to fly and to gather their own food. The infant bird is born a damp, cold-blooded animal. A brooding parent immediately gathers the chick to its body to dry it out, encourage growth and protect it until it makes a remarkable transition and becomes a warm-blooded creature. This transformation may take as little as two to seven hours, as among common eider ducks, which live and breed on the cold, foggy northern coasts, or as long as 21 days, as among cliff swallows of the milder temperate zones.

Parent birds must also devise a variety of ways to defend their hatchlings. Some, like terns, will threaten or attack an enemy, screeching and swooping until, only inches away, they wheel and fly off. Grouse have evolved a more effective defense: they signal their young to freeze until danger passes. Grebes carry away their threatened young on their backs.

Ultimately, however, fledglings must leave the nest. The tree duck calls to its offspring from the ground; the pygmy nuthatch pulls them from the nest hole; while the chachalaca actually carries them, clinging to its legs, from nest to earth.

COLLECTIVE CARE is practiced by emperor penguins after their young are big enough to gather in "kindergartens." Penguins are such avid brooders that they will fight to mother a stray.

INDIVIDUAL CARE characterizes the swan, seen here brooding its young. Although able to swim and feed themselves right after hatching, the young stay with adults some nine months.

WATTLES GLOWING in the sun, turkeys throng a Virginia corral where
they are fattened by scientific care
and feeding. About 100 million a
year now are raised in the United
States, over 170 times the estimated
population of turkeys in the wild.

8

Toward
a Balance
with Man

OF all the world's birds, none has had a more intimate association with man
nor contributed more to his welfare than the red jungle fowl, *Gallus gallus*.
From this one species of pheasant all the many varieties of domestic chickens
have had their origin and today the number of individuals runs into the billions,
making it by far the most numerous bird on earth—far more numerous, indeed,
than the human race. Although originating in the jungles and bamboo thickets
of southeastern Asia, it has penetrated to almost every corner of the world,
wherever man has taken root, except in frigid climates. Of all man's satellites
only dogs have become acclimated more widely.

We cannot quite be sure when men first took these fowl into their compounds and domesticated them, but it was probably more than 5,000 years
ago. *Gallus gallus* seems to have reached central Europe as early as 1500 B.C.
and was well established there by the time the Romans came. Long before the
white man's ships explored the Pacific, the Polynesians had carried fowl to the
Hawaiian Islands and wild variants of the original stock can still be seen in the
rain forest on Kauai. In fact, there has been recent evidence that the sea-going
Polynesians may have brought the first chickens to the New World.

FOUR FOUNDERS OF ORNITHOLOGY

COMTE DE BUFFON

Georges Louis Leclerc de Buffon (1707-1788), despite an unscientific tendency to humanize birds and animals, helped to establish ornithology as a science through his 10-volume, color-illustrated "Natural History of Birds" and his personal prestige as a member of the French court.

ALEXANDER WILSON

The Scottish-born Wilson (1766-1813) did not live to complete his projected 10-volume work on American birds. The eight volumes he finished, however, which were published before the work of his rival, Audubon, earned him the title of "the father of American ornithology."

Association with man has meant a sort of welfare state—protection and assurance of food—but the birds pay for this relative security with their eggs and their meat. While their wild brethren in the forest have remained virtually unchanged, the domestic birds have developed a hundred standard breeds or more. Through selection and special feeding some have become very much larger with heavier layers of meat. Egg laying has been increased to the point where champions may lay an egg nearly every day in the year.

While the hens were developed as egg factories, the natural pugnacity of the cocks appealed to the competitive instincts of some people and fighting strains with powerful legs and longer spurs were bred. Such birds bear a closer resemblance to their wild ancestors than most other breeds. But as man became more civilized he began to experiment with ornamental varieties. Here was a bird which was particularly plastic and, as William Beebe aptly put it, "the aesthetic side of mankind seized upon this as a sort of living, organic potter's clay." Some of the products of the fanciers' ingenuity are truly beautiful, others are bizarre, and some can only be described as monstrous. Giants and midgets have been bred, birds with stiltlike legs and others with absurdly stubby legs. There are crested varieties, frizzled fowl with every feather turning outward from the body and rumpless breeds. One of the most extraordinary (and also most useless) products of the breeder's art is the famous long-tailed fowl of Japan, the *Onagadori*, which has been known to attain tail feathers which are more than 20 feet in length.

Although ornamental breeders vie with each other, the main purpose of the thousands of poultry shows throughout the land is to improve the production of eggs or meat. In 1890 the 500-hen poultry farm was a source of wonder; today some farms boast 100,000 or more. In some of these poultry factories the chicken run has been eliminated and the "battery method" is used. Living a completely synthetic life the birds are raised entirely indoors in wire-bottom cages several shelves high, a far cry from the habitat of their jungle-bred ancestors.

In the United States poultry raising is now a multibillion dollar industry. The laying flock is sustained at around 300 million while nearly two billion are raised yearly as broilers. Egg production is in the neighborhood of 64 billion per year, nearly one egg a day for every man, woman and child in the United States.

Whereas the economic importance of chickens must be measured in billions of dollars, that of the 12 million domestic ducks marketed yearly in the United States amounts to only a few million. These are raised for their meat and most of them, even though they are sluggish, potbellied and white, are descended from the handsome, green-headed wild mallard. Wild ducks are far more important economically: pursued by nearly 1.5 million American sportsmen, most of whom not only pay three dollars apiece yearly for duck stamps, but also spend considerably more for equipment, travel and lodging, they support or help support a wide range of industries and services.

The turkey is America's great contribution to animal husbandry. The yearly hatch of poults often exceeds 100 million and it is almost certain that there are more turkeys in domestication today than ever roamed the primeval forest in pre-Columbian times. The Mexican race of the wild turkey had already been domesticated by the Indians when Mexico fell to Cortez. The returning conquistadors introduced the bird to Europe and by 1530 it was quite well established there, so when the Pilgrims celebrated their first Thanksgiving in

Massachusetts they undoubtedly were already familiar with the tasty fowl which the local Indians furnished for the feast.

It is a tossup whether chickens or pigeons are man's feathered associates of longest standing, but if we accept Biblical legend, Noah was the first pigeon fancier. Certainly the Egyptians raised pigeons for food and probably to carry messages as early as 3000 B.C., long before chickens reached the land of the Nile. Just when they were first used as a means of communication in war is not known, but Julius Caesar used them to send news of victory and they continued to play an important role as message bearers right down to World War II, when electronics finally largely supplanted their services.

Today pigeons are still raised by the millions throughout the world, as squabs to eat, for ornament and particularly for racing. More than 200 ornamental breeds are recognized. Pigeon racing, which has hundreds of thousands of devotees, was given a great impetus by the air age, which made it possible to transport birds hundreds of miles to their release points in a matter of hours.

THE progenitor of most, if not all, of the varieties of domestic pigeons is the rock dove, which still breeds wild on European sea cliffs. It is quite likely that wild birds first took to town life around the mosques and temples of southern Asia. Today most large cities have their self-sustaining flocks, for the high stone buildings are not unlike the ancestral sea cliffs.

Bird pets have probably graced the homes of men since the Bronze Age, but the cheerful canary, the very symbol of all cage birds, did not appear on the scene until the 16th Century, when seamen brought it from the Canary Islands to Europe. It proved to be as plastic as the jungle fowl and the rock dove, and selective breeding soon produced a variety of forms while training developed some very accomplished singers. To look at the ancestral canary, a streaky, olive-drab bird, and to hear it sing, one might think that the ordinary chaffinch of Europe would have been more promising material to work with.

It was not until the years after World War II that the supremacy of the canary was challenged by another cage bird, the little shell parakeet, or budgerigar. The millions in captivity now probably exceed the hordes that still throng the water holes of Australia's arid hinterland. In captivity they range from clear yellow to blue, but the wild ones are always green.

Aviculturists have multiplied even though protective laws in North America and in many countries of Europe prohibit them from cherishing, behind bars, most of the wild birds of their own countryside. So great has been the demand for some of the more attractive birds of faraway places that Kenya and other tropical countries have had to tighten their restrictions. The ornithologists and the fast-growing army of bird watchers, who prefer their birds wild and free to come and go, do not always see eye to eye with the cage bird clan. They contend that it contradicts the meaning of birds to possess them.

The most valuable wild bird in the world is certainly the guanay cormorant of coastal Peru. Although it cannot match the domestic fowl as a source of revenue, the value of its excrement amounts to millions of dollars every year. The Incas had used the rich nitrates for fertilizer since time immemorial but it was not until about 125 years ago that commercial exploitation made itself felt. Mountains of guano 150 feet deep, the accumulation of at least 25 centuries, were mined and shipped away. During the third quarter of the 19th Century Peru shipped 20 million tons of guano worth two billion dollars. With the depletion of these ancient reserves came sober management. The birds are now

JOHN JAMES AUDUBON

Audubon (1785-1851), who was primarily an artist, studied with the eminent painter David before he left France to live in America. His fame rests on his great folio of 435 plates, which were painted with unprecedented naturalness and accuracy from freshly killed bird specimens.

JOHN GOULD

Gould (1804-1881), who gained his reputation originally as a taxidermist, later became the leading bird illustrator of England. His first studies of Himalayan birds and hummingbirds, and his monumental "Birds of Europe," made a lasting contribution to the field of ornithology.

guarded, harvesting is regulated and new colonies are encouraged by platforms and retaining walls, all of which has resulted in an increment in the excrement.

Unbridled in their destruction, however, were the Mediterranean peoples who reduced the almost countless migratory quail to their present low level. These are the birds that saved the children of Israel from starvation, as related in Exodus, and it has been estimated by one researcher that in two days and one night they must have killed some nine million quail. But it was commercial exploitation and lack of conservation practices in more recent times that destroyed the big flocks. Prior to 1920 the Egyptians alone, in addition to home consumption, were exporting up to three million birds each year.

The modern philosophy that governs hunting is to crop the annual surplus but not dig into capital—to take the natural increase but not the "seed stock." Accompanying the much publicized population explosion of the human race has come increasing gun pressure, as well as pressure to add certain species to the game list. It is regrettable that the sandhill crane, a bird that lays but two eggs, is now allowed to be hunted locally. Shore birds, with their low reproductive potential (usually four eggs) and vulnerable migration lanes, were finally placed under protection, but not before the Eskimo curlew was brought to the very brink of extinction.

WATERFOWL, despite the fact that they lay large clutches and recover quickly from disaster if given a chance, face a future that looks far from bright. Unlike grouse, pheasants and quail that can spread themselves over hundreds of millions of American acres, they must concentrate where the water is. One leading professor of wildlife management predicts that duck hunting in the U.S. may go out within a generation. Many of us remember when the daily bag limit was 25 birds. Today it is down to two birds in some flyways.

We can do no more than guess at the original duck population of North America. Estimates run between 250 and 500 million. When the pioneer trapper Jim Bridger paddled his buffalo-skin canoe down the Bear River to Great Salt Lake in 1824, ducks darkened the sky in numbers this continent will never see again. He was soon followed by the market gunners who had already decimated the flocks in the East. In 1887 one gunner shot 1,880 birds in a season—another bagged 335 in one day.

The decline of the ducks, however, was not due solely to gun pressure, nor is it today. Virtually every day new plans were made somewhere to drain another pond or swamp or marsh, until about 50 million acres of the original 127 million acres of wetland in the United States had disappeared and millions of other acres were crisscrossed with mosquito-control ditches. In the duck-rich prairie provinces of Canada innumerable nesting places were drained, further diminishing the duck crop at its source. The dry cycle which created the dust bowl in the late 1920s had a disastrous effect on waterfowl. By 1935 the U.S. Fish and Wildlife Service estimated a continental population of only 27 million birds. It was during that period of deep depression that the great federal refuge program of the United States got under way. Today there are about 250 refuges specifically for waterfowl, covering an area of nearly four million acres. But in recent years the duck prairies have again been in the grip of a drought cycle, with lake bottoms blowing away in clouds of dust, and it is quite likely that the continental waterfowl population may be even lower than it was in 1935.

In an overcrowded world some forms of hunting, in the opinion of many conservationists, are rapidly becoming impractical and archaic and must eventually be replaced by just looking. How many people content themselves with looking at birds it is difficult to say, for they do not require licenses. Recently, when a survey was made at a Midwestern goose marsh, it was revealed that the goose hunters were outnumbered more than 100 to one by people who came just to see the geese.

As the human population soars above the three billion mark and on toward four billion, the clashes between birds and men are certain to become more frequent. The federal government is faced with many requests to control red-winged blackbirds, grackles and other seed-eating species that are having population explosions of their own—largely because they have adapted to changes in man's use of the land and now consider the vast wheat and corn fields as theirs to feed in. The growing army of people who like birds will not hear of such violent methods of control as poisoning, dynamiting or shooting, contending rightly that they are not selective enough and that other ways must be found to discourage bird depredations.

Birds have their own diseases which they transmit to other birds, but most of their maladies and their parasites do not affect man. Ornithosis, a sort of virus pneumonia harbored by birds (and once called psittacosis because it was thought to be a disease of parrots) can be transmitted to man by pigeons. But the ornithosis virus is not exclusive to birds—recently it was discovered in fur seals of the Bering Sea.

Among the most serious of the insect-borne viruses are several forms of encephalitis, or sleeping sickness, and it has been found that birds which are bitten by these insects often act as a reservoir of contagion. Thus when an outbreak occurs, the cry may go up to get rid of the birds, but this is clearly impractical. For one thing, the greatest offenders are domestic fowl, penned ducks and pheasants. But even if it were possible to eliminate all birds, wild and domestic, other vertebrate animals also can store the virus and infect humans. The problem must be handled in other ways and biologists and epidemiologists, working together, are seeking the answers.

WHAT of the future of birds? Taking the long, evolutionary view, we might surmise that some birds may go out of the picture, not simply because modern man has made an ecological nuisance of himself, eliminating their habitat, the source of their livelihood, but because they have reached a cul-de-sac, a dead end out of the main stream of life in a changing world. This could be the predicament of the California condor. With a surviving population of some two score individuals, this is the last descendant of the giant scavenger that flourished in North America during the Pleistocene, when mammals were bigger and more abundant than they are today.

Sixty or 70 million years ago, judging by the fossil evidence, the Gruiformes (cranes, rails, bustards and their relatives) made up a far larger part of the world's avifauna than they do today. In addition, they have also declined faster in historic times than any other major order. But whereas the cranes and certain other orders of large birds—the ostrich, the other ratites, and the pelican-like birds—may be slowly losing ground, the perching birds, which make up more than three fifths of all the world's birds, seem to have had their greatest proliferation within the past 10 million years, since the early Pliocene.

Among the perching birds, the seedeaters—the weaverbirds, sparrows, finches and their allies—are the most numerous and perhaps the most plastic. They came into their own relatively recently when seed-bearing plants, especially

A PLURALITY OF BIRDS

Over the years men have coined a host of special terms to describe birds in groups. Here are some that still survive in the English language.

a siege of herons or bitterns
a plump of wildfowl
a gaggle of geese
a skein of geese (flying)
a herd of swans, cranes or curlews
a badelyng of ducks
a sord (or sute) of mallards
a spring of teal
a company of widgeon
a cast of hawks
a bevy of quail
a covey of partridges
a muster of peacocks
a nye of pheasants
a brood of chickens
a covert of coots
a congregation of plovers
a desert of lapwings
a wisp (or walk) of snipe
a fall of woodcock
a bazaar of murres (guillemots)
a flight of doves or swallows
a murmuration of starlings
an exaltation of larks
a watch of nightingales
a building of rooks
a chattering of choughs
a host of sparrows

grasses and sedges, had their great spread. It has been suggested that of all birds they probably have the most promising future, but equal claims could be made for the insect eaters or the nectar feeders. They are all in the same business, evolving along with the flowering plants.

If the average turnover, the life of a species, is about 500,000 years, as Pierce Brodkorb estimates for the Pleistocene, the rate of extinction and replacement in the evolutionary sense should not be more than two species per century. If we accept Brodkorb's yardstick the world should have lost during the past three centuries, since the twilight of the dodo, five or six species through no fault of our own. Indeed, the Labrador duck might well have been one of these, for we cannot truly blame its disappearance on any known human activity.

However, during the past three centuries, or more precisely since 1680, we have lost nearly 80 species, some of which are not even represented by a specimen in any of the world's museums. Extinction, if we use Brodkorb's measure, has thus proceeded at about 15 times the evolutionary pace. (James Fisher, assuming a more telescoped time scale in recent millennia, feels that this estimate is excessive, but admits that man-induced extinction may have been as much as four times as great as it would have been had nature gone its own course.) The years of greatest loss were around the turn of the century. In the 20 years between 1885 and 1905, some 20 species became extinct. Most of the extinctions were among island birds, for they are more vulnerable than continental species. Some, like the dodo and the great auk, being unable to fly were ruthlessly killed off; others disappeared because of the introduction of rats, goats, cats, rabbits and the mongoose, satellites of man which have swept island after island like a scourge. Still others went out when their special environments were destroyed for agricultural use. Not a small number, such as some of the famous Hawaiian honey creepers, disappeared very mysteriously, but there is some evidence that they may have succumbed to diseases carried by introduced birds—bird malaria and bird sleeping sickness. These are diseases to which the invaders might well have built up a tolerance, but which the native birds could not throw off any more than the native Polynesians could withstand the ravages of measles and other "harmless" diseases brought by Captain Cook and other early infection-carrying visitors to their islands.

NORTH AMERICA has lost the great auk, Labrador duck, Carolina parakeet, passenger pigeon and the heath hen, a subspecies of the prairie chicken. But Europe, settled more slowly, has not lost a single mainland species in historic times (the great auk was an island bird). Normally, birds of continental range can cushion the shock of the invader and survive somewhere in the hinterland, perhaps adapting in time; but birds of the islands when pressed soon have their backs to the sea.

A handful of other birds is so close to extinction that we cannot be sure whether they will survive from one decade to the next. If we were to draw up a roster of endangered species we might easily have a world list of 100 or more. We have already mentioned some of them on our own continent north of the Mexican boundary—the ivory-billed woodpecker, the Eskimo curlew, the tall whooping crane and the California condor. Elsewhere in the world, the short-tailed albatross is making a slow recovery after having been all but wiped out on Japan's Bonin Islands; the noisy scrub bird of Australia, the cahow of Bermuda and the notornis of New Zealand, all on the brink of the void, are now under rigid protection after having been rediscovered in recent years.

GONE WITH THE WIND

GREAT AUK

The great auk, first bird recorded extinct in the Western Hemisphere, was a goose-sized island dweller of the North Atlantic. Although flightless, it was an excellent swimmer and could have survived indefinitely had it not been ruthlessly hunted by men over a period of 300 years. The last known specimens, a breeding pair, were killed in Iceland in 1844.

LABRADOR DUCK

Little is known about the disappearance of the Labrador duck. Its numbers were apparently small to begin with; then, between 1850 and 1870, it dwindled and vanished. During that time it was hunted, but not excessively. Whether disease, shooting or the loss of some vital food caused its extinction has never been determined, and almost certainly never will be.

There is a finality about extinction. We can often place a precise date on the disappearance of a bird, but we cannot do the same with an emergent species; it takes its time. That is why the experts often disagree as to whether a bird is a "good" species (i.e., reproductively isolated) or worthy only of subspecific rank.

Alexander Wilson, the father of American ornithology, anticipated more than 150 years ago that the ivory-billed woodpecker, dependent on primeval wilderness, would disappear. He intimated that the other crow-sized woodpecker, the pileated, would follow it, but in this he erred. The genetic stock that could exist in cut-over forest survived to replenish areas which had not heard the loud tapping of the "logcock" in more than a generation. Today it is again a fairly common bird.

The birds that could adapt to gardens, towns, orchards, roadsides and farms are the ones that have prospered most—robins, song sparrows, chipping sparrows, yellow warblers, house wrens, mockingbirds, cardinals, blue jays, meadowlarks, orioles, grackles, kingbirds, phoebes and at least two or three dozen others. The swallows, as a family, have completely accepted man as a benefactor: barn swallows and cliff swallows prefer his barns and bridges to the cliffs and caves they formerly used; tree swallows and martins use his bird boxes, and bank swallows colonize the sand quarries and road cuts. Swifts find chimneys preferable to hollow trees; nighthawks lay their eggs on the flat roofs of office buildings; and so we might go on down the list of successfully integrated bird neighbors.

I T is quite certain that as our cities mature the shade trees and gardens will harbor more birds, not fewer. In England, an older country, the highest densities of birds, as we have seen, are in suburban gardens and estates, averaging about 30 birds per acre, or far more than optimum woodland densities.

We need not worry about the future of most songbirds, provided we do not exterminate them with chemical insecticides. The birds that will need our indulgence most are those that require ample living space, like the bald eagle and other birds that have very special requirements.

It is ironic that the most abundant wild bird the world has ever known should have become the very symbol of extinction. The passenger pigeon, estimated to number perhaps five billion in the days of Audubon and Wilson, had a population nearly as great as that of all other breeding land birds in the United States combined. Although the last wild bird was shot in March, 1900 a few lived on in captivity until Martha, the lone survivor, died in the Cincinnati Zoo on September 1, 1914, at 1 p.m. Central Standard Time.

Since the beginning of the century, when the slaughter of the commercially prized plume birds and the murder of Guy Bradley, the Audubon warden who sought to stop it, had become a national shame, America has set an example to the world for its progress in bird protection. No country has better protective laws, more bird clubs, more graduate students seeking degrees in ornithology, more millions of acres set aside as refuges, or spends more money each year for conservation.

Throughout the rest of the world, the pattern of bird awareness and protection is uneven. Whereas it is strong in the United States and Canada, in some of the Latin American countries it is almost nonexistent. This ethnic division finds a parallel in western Europe, where bird watching is popular in such places as England, Holland, Germany and Scandinavia, but not in the

CAROLINA PARAKEET

This bird, the only parrot native to the United States, was also a victim of man's predation. A habit of twisting green fruit off the trees led to its widespread destruction as a nuisance. As the country was settled, its original wide range, extending throughout the southern states, steadily contracted, and a flock of 30 in Florida, in 1920, was the last that was ever seen.

HEATH HEN

The last heath hen, a mateless male, died on Martha's Vineyard, Mass. in 1932. Once plentiful around New York and southern New England, this bird could not survive coexistence with men. The settling of the land, plus wholesale shooting for the market, helped decimate it during the end of the 19th Century. Stringent measures to protect it came too late.

Mediterranean basin, where people appreciate birds more in the cage or in the skillet. Among eastern peoples the interest in birds and their conservation reaches its nadir in the Arab countries and its highest degree of development in progressive Japan.

Recently, something like a national policy with respect to birds has been evolving in the U.S., but its outlines are contradictory. Dr. Joseph J. Hickey of the University of Wisconsin points out: "Without a permit you cannot pick up and take home a car-killed Baltimore oriole, but you can, generally with impunity, cut down a tree containing an oriole nest full of young. You cannot shoot a snowy egret, but you can drain off a marsh on which a whole colony of egret nestlings may depend for food. You cannot shoot a robin, but you can kill it with insecticides."

This inconsistency has become tragically clear since World War II and particularly during the last 10 years, when pesticides have been widely promoted, like wonder drugs, as a panacea for all conceivable insect ills and plant diseases. George Wallace, Professor of Zoology at Michigan State University, in describing the potential effect of indiscriminate spraying on bird life, went so far as to call it "worse than deforestation, worse than market gunning, worse than drainage, drought or oil pollution. . . . If the pest eradication programs are carried out as now projected we shall have been witness within a single decade to a greater extermination of animal life than in all the previous years of man's history."

Eventually birds will return to despoiled areas, providing they are not sprayed again, but orchards given the yearly treatment suffer permanent loss. To bluebirds, now scarce, the spraying of orchards has been a disaster.

More subtle than the immediate results of spraying are the residual effects. Earthworms ingesting leaf mold months after elms have been sprayed with DDT against the Dutch elm disease accumulate the poisons in their bodies. Ten such infected worms may be enough to kill a robin, but the mass dying may not occur until the spring after the spraying.

Noting that the resident robin population on the Michigan State campus dropped from 370 to three in a period of only four years, Wallace asserted that "millions" of robins must have died in the effort to save the elm trees of the Midwest. Wisconsin's Hickey, more conservative, estimated that up to half a million robins were killed when DDT was first used on elms in the Middle West, plus somewhat lesser numbers in succeeding years.

Fish, like earthworms, also store DDT and other hydrocarbon poisons in their tissues and because of this it is possible that the bald eagle and the osprey, both fisheaters, may disappear from the Atlantic coast within the next decade or two. The birds now sit for weeks on unhatched eggs and few young are raised—on analysis, both osprey and eagle eggs have shown significant amounts of the life-destroying chemicals.

The public has finally been alerted to the risks, and a great deal of research is now under way to find substitutes for the dangerous poisons being used. More selective chemicals may be the answer, as well as biological controls. Disease, predators and parasites are nature's way of handling overpopulation; we should take advantage of these natural controls and use chemicals only when they do not destroy nature's own regulatory mechanisms. Certainly a world without birds or a spring without song would be incomplete for any man; for many of us it would be intolerable.

OSTRICHES RUN ACROSS A ROCK IN THE SAHARA, PRESERVED FOR THE AGES BY SOME STONE AGE ARTIST AT LEAST 10,000 YEARS AGO

Man, the Admiring Enemy

Man's association with birds has always been peculiarly intimate, if one-sided. He has worshiped birds, used them as symbols in his art, hunted them for food and plumage, and watched 78 species disappear in modern times. But while exploiting them, he has also defended them. Today, with birds threatened as never before, he is helping some of them with their greatest problem: living with man.

IN A SCENE FAMILIAR TO ANY HUNTER, AN EGYPTIAN MURAL SHOWS DUCKS TAKING WING, TWO HIT BY STICKS, AND A HERON DECOY (LEFT)

THE WISE OLD OWL was first so named by the Greeks, who pictured it as the companion of Athene, goddess of wisdom. Here an owl appears on an Athenian coin of the Fifth Century B.C.

Birds as Gods and Symbols

In ancient civilizations, birds were symbols often raised to the rank of deities. Probably the original bird god was the Garuda, a great, golden-winged mythical eagle of Tibet, "the bird of life, destroyer of all, creator of all." The Babylonians and the Hittites built temples to eagles. The strongest deity of the Egyptian pantheon was Horus, a falcon. Minor Egyptian gods, both benevolent and evil, were also represented in bird form, like the pintails shown above in a detail from a 15th Century B.C. tomb. The ducks being flushed from a papyrus marsh symbolize demons which are ritually struck down by throwing sticks carved in the shape of serpents. Other birds were also given supernatural powers in many societies: the priests of Rome considered it a bad omen before a battle if the sacred chickens showed little appetite for their ceremonial grain.

A HAWAIIAN WAR IDOL IS DECORATED WITH RED IIWI FEATHERS AND BLACK OO FEATHERS

Where Feathers Buy a Bride

Man has always treasured the bright plumage of many birds, but in the modern world only one place still uses them as actual currency: Santa Cruz island, an Australian trust territory in the South Pacific. In the island's economy, this exotic money, in the form of woven feather belts, is interchangeable with the Australian pound. The value of the belts is standardized by the fixed price of a Santa Cruz bride: 10 belts of varying quality, ranging from a brand-new, bright-red belt worth £25 down to a faded gray one worth one shilling.

The bird that supplies the money is the tiny honey eater, from whose scarlet feathers the belts are woven. Its strange role in the island's economy may seem to be a threat to its existence, but in this case there are stronger economic forces at work: beltmakers have dwindled to fewer than half the number working a decade ago; and as more Australian money flows into the island, rising labor costs force them to demand higher prices for their belts than they can get. Result: Fewer belts are being made; fewer feathers are needed; honey eaters are thriving.

A LIVE HONEY EATER is tied to a stick to lure other males which will attack their helpless fellow and get stuck on gummy latex smeared on the perch. It takes 300 birds to make one feather belt.

A STRING OF BIRDS is brought in by the snarer for plucking. He will sell the feathers, tightly packed into a coconut shell, to the man who begins the process of making the money (right).

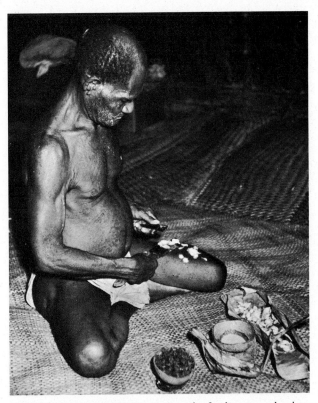

MANUFACTURE OF MONEY starts as the feathers are glued to small plaques made of pigeon feathers. The plaques are then sold to other craftsmen who bind them into belts 30 feet long.

COILED BELTS OF FEATHER MONEY ARE CHECKED FOR PROPER VALUE BY THE FAMILY OF A PROSPECTIVE BRIDE

FRANTIC RHEAS, MILLING IN THE TRAP, MUST BE CAUGHT AND WRESTLED TO THE GROUND ONE BY ONE, A HAZARDOUS AND EXHAUSTING TASK

Roundup Time for Rheas

Like the Santa Cruz islanders, certain gauchos of southeastern Brazil's cattle country are hunters of plumage—but with a difference. Their quarry is the rhea, South American cousin of the ostrich. The plumage they seek is the rhea's tail feathers, sold in Brazil and Argentina as feather dusters; the birds, far from dying, grow another set of feathers and live to be plucked again. In fact, the ranchers who let the gauchos hunt protect the rheas because they keep down snakes and rodents.

The rhea roundup runs through May and June. Traveling across the flat Texas-like campo in teams of six, the gauchos scout a herd of rheas and set up their net traps. Then, cowboy-style, they drive the rheas into the trap, subdue them and pluck their plumage—taking care to keep clear of the big bird's kick, which can break a man's arm. In two months, a six-man team makes enough money to enable these roving cowboy-huntsmen to live in comfort around their campfires for the next 10 months.

A BARE-RUMPED RHEA, its plumes gone (*right*), bounds to the safety of the open campo. With a top speed of 45 miles an hour, a five-foot rhea can briefly outrun a horse.

A HANDFUL OF FEATHERS is yanked by a grinning gaucho from the tail of a shocked and panting rhea. A fair catch for a six-man team is about 60 birds per day.

DODOS WERE DRAWN IN 1599 BY A DUTCH ARTIST WHO MAY HAVE HAD SPECIMENS TO WORK FROM. NO COMPLETE SPECIMEN REMAINS TODAY

IGNORANCE about dodos is revealed by these drawings which agree only on heavy body, big bill and feet.

The Ultimate Doom

The rhea and the honey eater are two birds that have withstood the ravages of man. The Mauritius dodo and the American passenger pigeon are two that have not. The dodo, first bird to become extinct in modern times, was doomed by inability to fly when man brought pigs and rats to Mauritius in the 16th Century. Much of its life and habits are a mystery, but it was a sluggish bird, easy prey for these hunters and eaters of its eggs. The last dodo vanished at the end of the 17th Century.

The passenger pigeon died more quickly and more ominously. Early in the 19th Century, North America still supported three to five billion of these birds, far more than any other species on the continent. They were esteemed for their delicate flavor; their crowded nesting grounds and communal flights made them easy prey to wholesale shooting and netting. By 1880 it was already too late to save them. The last wild passenger pigeon was shot in 1900; the last of them all died in captivity in 1914.

MARTHA

last of her species, died at 1:00 p.m.,
1 September 1914, age 29, in the
Cincinnati Zoological Gardens.

EXTINCT

THE END OF A SPECIES that used to darken American skies with flocks of millions came on September 1, 1914, when Martha, the last passenger pigeon, died in the Cincinnati zoo. Her stuffed body is now in the National Museum in Washington *(above)*, a sad reminder that once a species begins to die out, the dying may snowball at a rate that even an aroused public cannot stop.

THE MOST MAJESTIC BIRD in North America, a whooping crane may exceed five feet and attain a seven-foot wing span.

On the Brink of Extinction

The extinction of the passenger pigeon dramatized what ornithologists have now bitterly learned: many birds cannot adjust to man. If such species are to survive, man must adjust to them and take active, even drastic measures to protect them. A case in point is the whooping crane. This large, aristocratic bird—named for its loud, buglelike call and famous for its graceful mating dance—once flew in sizable numbers from its winter retreat on the Gulf of Mexico to its breeding grounds on the Great Plains. There it built grass nests one or two feet high in marshes and shallow lakes. But with the westward surge of man during the last two decades of the 19th Century, whooping cranes were gradually crowded

ONE DAY OLD, A BABY WHOOPING CRANE IN THE NEW ORLEANS AUDUBON PARK ZOO IS FED INSECTS BY ITS PARENTS. A FULL-GROWN CRANE

out of their breeding areas. Many of the swamps where they nested were drained. Many cranes were indiscriminately shot on their migratory flights. By 1889, they had deserted their last nesting sites in Minnesota and by 1940 they were down to a pitiful handful of about 20 birds that wintered in the coastal marshes of Texas. Nobody knew where these birds laid their eggs. Then, in 1955, they were discovered nesting in northern Alberta. Now, more than 40 of them migrate each year from this remote area to their winter home in Texas, carefully protected in both places and en route. But they, plus seven in captivity, are the last of their species. For many years it will be touch and go whether they survive.

HAS A DIET THAT INCLUDES WORMS, FROGS, SNAKES AND SHELLFISH

SIX WEEKS OLD, a baby whooping crane's immature body perches precariously on stiltlike legs. As an adult, its long windpipe will be trumpeting a cry that can be heard for two miles.

183

A Helpful Hand for Storks

Though the European stork is the traditional baby-deliverer for people, it is having surprising difficulty maintaining its own population. Long a fixture of European towns, where it nests on chimneys and steeples, the stork is now declining. Holland had 312 breeding couples in 1939, only 50 in 1955. Switzerland had 150 couples in 1900; in 1949 it had none.

No one is certain why the storks' survival rate is dropping, though it may be the growing use of insecticides in South Africa, where the storks migrate to feed on grasshoppers and other insects in winter. Whatever the cause, the bird lovers of Alsace, whose people consider the stork a symbol of good luck, are determined to stop it. They have set up a committee to help the storks and have called in ornithologists to teach villagers how to build and renovate nests. They have even imported stork eggs from North Africa and hatched them in incubators.

A similar dedication to the preservation of birds is growing in many lands. Wildlife conservation has become much more urgent with the spread of metropolitan areas. In North America, where four species have died out since the white man came, four to five million bird watchers are now concerned with the protection of the 650 species that still breed there.

MAN-MADE NEST, on the unfinished roof of Ilhaeusern church in Alsace, was built for storks by the villagers when the church was rebuilt from the rubble of war. Storks return to it year after year to raise families.

 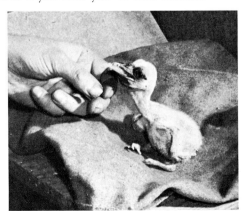 

WORK OF PRESERVATION in Alsace includes building nests *(left)*, care and feeding of stork chicks hatched in incubators by local protectionists and even propagation of their favorite local food, frogs. The sign above, hung in restaurants of the area, requests diners not to ask for frogs' legs but to please "leave this delicacy for our young"—and is signed "the storks of Alsace."

AT DAWN IN WASHINGTON, D.C., ORNITHOLOGISTS BEGIN A BIRD COUNT. THE AUTHOR IS SECOND FROM LEFT

Credits

Credits for pictures from left to right are separated by commas, top to bottom by dashes.

PHOTOGRAPHS—Cover: Robert B. Goodman from Black Star 17: Georg Nystrand from Frank Lane 20: Robert B. Goodman from Black Star 21: Cy La Tour 22: Ron Austing from Photo Researchers, Inc.—Constance P. Warner 23: John Markham 24,25: Dmitri Kessel 26,27: N. R. Farbman, Jerry Cooke from Photo Researchers, Inc., John Markham from Photo Researchers, Inc. 28: John Markham 29: Christina Loke from *Birds in the Sun* by Malcolm MacDonald from Photo Researchers, Inc. 30,31: John Markham from Photo Researchers, Inc. 32: Robert B. Goodman from Black Star 41: Andreas Feininger 46,47: Andreas Feininger 48: Tokutaro Tanaka 49: Martin Iger for SPORTS ILLUSTRATED 50,51: Constance P. Warner 52: R. Van Nostrand from National Audubon Society 53: Lilo Hess except top left; Marie Hansen 54: Rene-Pierre Bille except top; Leon D. Harmon from Photo Researchers, Inc. 55: Hans W. Silvester 56: J. Bristol Foster 66,67: Kurt Severin 68: Hermann Schunemann from Annan Photo Service except bottom; Heinz Sielmann 69: Christina Loke from *Birds in the Sun* by Malcolm MacDonald from Photo Researchers, Inc. 70 through 73: Shelly Grossman 74,75: Fritz Goro, James Simon from Photo Researchers, Inc.—Roger Tory Peterson—Maitland A. Edey 76: Constance P. Warner 78: John G. Zimmerman 89,92: Eric Hosking from Photo Researchers, Inc. 93: Roger Tory Peterson 94,95: Robert Cushman Murphy 96,97: Hans W. Silvester 98: Eric Schaal 109: Eric Hosking from Photo Researchers, Inc. 110,111: James Whitmore 112,113: John G. Zimmerman 114: Georg Nystrand 115: William J. Johoda from National Audubon Society, J. R. Eyerman—Albert Fenn 116,117: Leonard McCombe 118: David Goodnow 120: Leonard W. Wing from *Natural History of Birds, a Guide to Ornithology,* © 1956, The Ronald Press Company—Aretas A. Saunders from *A Guide to Bird Songs,* © 1935 d Appleton-Century Crofts, Inc.—Wesley E. Lanyon, The American Museum of Natural History 127: Treat Davidson from National Audubon Society 130,131: Helen Cruickshank from National Audubon Society 132,133: Jane Burton 134: Leonard Lee Rue 3rd from Monkmeyer Press Photos—O. S. Pettingill, Jr.. from National Audubon Society, Roger Tory Peterson 135: Jack Dermid 136: Walther Rohdich from Annan Photo Service 147: Christopher Doncaster 148,149: Niall Rankin 150,151: Warren Roth from Black Star 152: Gordon A. Ranger courtesy of H. Friedman—Eric Hosking from Photo Researchers, Inc. 153: John Markham 154,155: Jack J. Kunz 156,157: Christina Loke from *Birds in the Sun* by Malcolm MacDonald from Photo Researchers, Inc., Loke Wan Tho, Christina Loke from *Birds in the Sun* by Malcolm MacDonald from Photo Researchers, Inc.—William H. Drury, Jr., B. Max Thompson from National Audubon Society 158,159: Helen Cruickshank from National Audubon Society, Walter Dawn 160: Torrey Jackson from Photo Researchers, Inc. 161: L. H. Smith from Len Sirman Press 162,163: Russ Kinne from Photo Researchers, Inc., Robert Doisneau from Rapho Guillumette 164: Alfred Eisenstaedt 173: Emil Schulthess courtesy Conzett and Huber from Black Star 174: Abeille document from *Great Centuries of Painting—Egyptian Painting,* editions Skira Geneva—Charles Mohr from National Audubon Society 175,176,177: William Davenport, Yale University 178,179: E. A. Gourley 180: Charles Muskavitch 181: Noel Clark 182,183: Joe Scherschel except top left; Red Moores 184: Thomas D. McAvoy 185: Francis Miller

PAINTINGS AND DRAWINGS—81: Mark A. Binn 35,102,103 (maps), 106, 107: Adolph E. Brotman 12,13,34,36 through 39,59,60,61,82,83,123, 125: Lois and Louis Darling 128, 129 (landscape): Ara Derderian 90, 91: Bill Dove 8, 42, 43, 44, 45 (ducks based on pen and camera studies by Richard E. Bishop and Edgar M. Queeny in *Prairie Wings;* hummingbirds based on drawings by Dale Astle in *Hummingbirds*), 166, 167: Rudolf Freund 154, 155: Jack J. Kunz 15: René Martin 62, 140, 141: Peter Parnell 10, 11, 18, 19, 86, 87, 102, 103 (birds), 128, 129 (birds), 143, 144, 145, 170, 171, back cover: Roger Tory Peterson

Acknowledgments

The editors of this book are particularly indebted to Eugene Eisenmann, Research Associate, Department of Ornithology, The American Museum of Natural History, who read the book in its entirety, and to Andrew J. Berger, Associate Professor of Anatomy, University of Michigan; Roland C. Clement, Staff Biologist, National Audubon Society; James Fisher, Director and Chief Editor, Rathbone Books, London; and Robert J. Newman, Curator, Museum of Zoology, Louisiana State University, who read and criticized the chapters in their special areas.

The editors are also indebted to John Aldrich, U.S. Fish and Wildlife Service; Arthur Allen, Cornell University; Dean Amadon, The American Museum of Natural History; Pierce Brodkorb, University of Florida; the late James Chapin, The American Museum of Natural History; William Conway, New York Zoological Park; Philip A. DuMont and Allan Duvall, U.S. Fish and Wildlife Service; Crawford H. Greenewalt and Doubleday and Co. for permission to use *Hummingbirds* as source for drawings on pages 44 and 45; Mary Heimerdinger, Yale University; Joseph J. Hickey, University of Wisconsin; Peter Paul Kellogg, Cornell University; Jane Kinne, Photo Researchers, Inc.; Wesley E. Lanyon, Robert Cushman Murphy and Charles E. O'Brien, The American Museum of Natural History; Barbara Peterson; A. H. and A. W. Reed, publishers, New Zealand; S. Dillon Ripley, Secretary of the Smithsonian Institution; Charles G. Sibley, Cornell University; John H. Storer; Niko Tinbergen, Oxford University, England; Joel Carl Welty, Beloit College; Robert Woodward, National Audubon Society; Rhea Zinman, U.S. Department of Agriculture; the Patuxent Research Refuge, U.S. Fish and Wildlife Service; and the library staffs of The American Museum of Natural History and the National Audubon Society.

The author also thanks the following who furnished data for the map pages 90-91: Gordon Alcorn, Washington; Robert Arbib, New York; Alfred M. Bailey, Colorado; James L. Baillie, Ontario; Joyce A. Bates, Vermont; William H. Behle, Utah; Alexander Bergstrom, Connecticut; Francisco Bernis, Spain; James Bond, West Indies; Maurice Brooks, West Virginia; John L. Bull, New Jersey; Thomas D. Burleigh, Idaho; Joseph Cadbury, New Jersey; Roland C. Clement, Rhode Island; Ben B. Coffey, Jr., Tennessee; Howard L. Cogswell, California; I. McTagart Cowan, British Columbia; Kai Curry-Lindahl, Sweden; David Cutler, New Jersey; Clifford V. Davis, Montana; L. Irvy Davis, Mexico; David A. Easterla, Kansas; Ruth Emery, Massachusetts; Robert B. Etchecopar, France; James Fisher, Great Britain, U.S.S.R.; Sergio Frugis, Italy; Robert W. Fuller, Vermont; Mrs. Robert Gammell, North Dakota; B. E. Gandy, Mississippi; Albert F. Ganier, Tennessee; Paul Geroudet, Switzerland, France, Germany; Bruce Glick, Mississippi; W. Earl Godfrey, Alberta, Quebec, Labrador, Prince Edward Island, New Brunswick, Northwest Territories, Yukon; Richard R. Graber, Illinois; Finnur Gudmundsson, Iceland; Gordon Gunter, Mississippi; Dr. Henry D. Haberyan, Mississippi; Earl H. Hath, Missouri; Mrs. Richard C. Hebert, New Hampshire; Joseph J. Hickey, Wisconsin; Julian Hill, Delaware; Holger Holgersen, Norway; P.A.D. Hollom, Great Britain, Ireland, Europe; Stuart Houston, Saskatchewan; Laurence P. Howe, Vermont; Dr. Joseph C. Howell, Tennessee; Douglas James, Arkansas; Ned K. Johnson, Nevada; Brina Kessel, Alaska; Edgar Kincaid, Texas; J. Kist, Holland; Donald E. Kunkle, New Jersey; Harrison F. Lewis, Nova Scotia; Bernt Löppenthin, Denmark; Carl-Frederick Lundevall, Sweden; Locke L. Mackenzie, Connecticut; David B. Marshal, Oregon; Joseph T. Marshall, Jr., Arizona; Robert M. Mengel, Kentucky; Marion F. Metcalf, Vermont; Burt L. Monroe, Sr., Kentucky; Russell E. Mumford, Indiana; Reverend J. J. Murray, Virginia; Robert J. Niedrach, Colorado; G. Niethammer, Germany; Ralph Palmer, Maine; Kenneth C. Parkes, Pennsylvania; Peter Petersen, Iowa; Fred J. Pierce, Iowa; Tudor Richards, New Hampshire; Frank Richardson, Nevada; S. Dillon Ripley, India and Pakistan; Chandler Robbins, Jr., Maryland; William B. Robertson, Jr., Florida; Gerth Rokitansky, Austria; W. Rydzewski, Poland; Oliver K. Scott, Wyoming; Marion Smith, Vermont; Wendell Smith, Vermont; Dorothy E. Snyder, Massachusetts; Alexander Sprunt, Jr., South Carolina; James D. Stewart, Vermont; Herbert L. Stoddard, Sr., Georgia; Finn Salomonsen, Denmark, Greenland; Arnold Small, California; George M. Sutton, Oklahoma; M. J. Tekke, Holland; Edward S. Thomas, Ohio; Harrison B. Tordoff, Michigan; Milton B. Trautman, Ohio; Leslie M. Tuck, Newfoundland; Harold F. Tufts, Nova Scotia; Charles Vaurie, China, Korea, Outer Mongolia; Dwain W. Warner, Minnesota; N. R. Whitney, South Dakota.

Bibliography

Biology of Birds, General

Berger, Andrew J., *Bird Study*. John Wiley and Sons, 1961.

Darling, Lois and Louis, *Bird*. Houghton Mifflin, 1962.

Fisher, James, *Watching Birds*. Penguin Books, 1946.

Fisher, James, and Roger Tory Peterson, *The World of Birds*. Doubleday, 1964.

Marshall, Alexander J., ed., *Biology and Comparative Physiology of Birds* (2 vols.). Academic Press, 1960, 1961.

Pettingill, Olin S., Jr., *Laboratory and Field Manual of Ornithology*. Burgess, 1956.

Stefferud, Alfred, and Arnold L. Nelson, *Birds in Our Lives*. U.S. Dept. of the Interior, 1966.

Thomson, Landsborough, *A New Dictionary of Birds*. McGraw-Hill, 1964.

Van Tyne, J., and A. J. Berger, *Fundamentals of Ornithology*. John Wiley and Sons, 1959.

Wallace, George J., *An Introduction to Ornithology*. Macmillan, 1955.

Welty, Joel Carl, *The Life of Birds*. Knopf, 1963.

Evolution and Classification

American Ornithologists Union, *Check-list of North American Birds* (5th ed.). 1957.

Eisenmann, Eugene, *The Species of Middle American Birds*. Linnaean Society, 1955.

Fisher, James, *A History of Birds*. Hutchinson, 1954.

Mayr, Ernst, *Animal Species and Evolution*. Harvard University Press, 1963.

Mayr, Ernst, and Dean Amadon, *A Classification of Recent Birds*. American Museum of Natural History, 1951.

Meyer de Schauensee, R., *The Species of Birds of South America*. Livingston, 1966.

Peters, J. L., *Check-list of Birds of the World* (9 vols.). Harvard University Press, 1931-1960.

Ridgway, R., and H. Friedmann, *Birds of North and Middle America* (11 vols.). U.S. National Museum, 1901-1950.

Ripley, S. Dillon, *A Synopsis of the Birds of India and Pakistan*. Bombay Natural History Soc., 1961.

Vaurie, Charles, *The Birds of the Palearctic Fauna* (Volumes I and II). Witherby, 1959, 1965.

Wetmore, Alexander, *A Classification for the Birds of the World* (Vol. 139 [11], 1-37). Smithsonian Misc. Collection, 1960.

Regional Books and Guides

Austin, Oliver L., Jr., and Arthur Singer, *Birds of the World*. Golden Press, 1961.

Blake, Emmet R., *Birds of Mexico*. University of Chicago Press, 1953.

Bond, James, *Birds of the West Indies*. Houghton Mifflin, 1960.

Cayley, N. W., *What Bird Is That? A Guide to the Birds of Australia*. Angus and Robertson, 1931.

Dementiev, T. N., and H. A. Gladkov, *Birds of the Soviet Union* (6 vols.). Moscow, State Publication, 1951-1954 (in Russian).

Gilliard, E. T., *Living Birds of the World*. Doubleday, 1958.

Godfrey, W. Earl, *The Birds of Canada*. National Museum of Canada, 1966.

Mackworth-Praed, C. W., and C.H.B. Grant, *Birds of Eastern and Northeastern Africa* (2 vols.). Longmans Green, 1952-1955.

Meyer de Schauensee, R., *The Birds of Colombia*. Livingston, 1964.

Murphy, R. C., and D. Amadon, *Land Birds of America*. McGraw-Hill, 1953.

Palmer, Ralph, *Handbook of North American Birds* (Vol. I). Yale University Press, 1962.

Peterson, Roger Tory, *A Field Guide to the Birds*. Houghton Mifflin, 1947.

Peterson, Roger Tory, *A Field Guide to Western Birds*. Houghton Mifflin, 1961.

Peterson, R.T., G. Mountfort, and P.A.D. Hollom, *A Field Guide to the Birds of Britain and Europe*. Houghton Mifflin, 1954.

Pettingill, O. S., Jr., *A Guide to Bird Finding* (2 vols., east and west of the Mississippi). Oxford University Press, 1951, 1953.

Pough, R. H., *Audubon Bird Guide: Eastern Landbirds; Water Birds* (2 vols.). Doubleday, 1946-1951.

Pough, R. H., *Audubon Western Bird Guide*. Doubleday, 1957.

Robbins, Chandler, Bertel Bruun, Herbert S. Zim and Arthur B. Singer, *Birds of North America*. Golden Press, 1966.

Roberts, A., *The Birds of South Africa*. Revised edition. Cape Times Ltd., 1957.

Voous, Karel H., *Atlas of European Birds*. Nelson, 1961.

Witherby, H. F., ed., *The Handbook of British Birds* (5 vols.). Witherby, 1943.

Life Histories

Bannerman, David A., *The Birds of the British Isles* (10 vols.). Oliver and Boyd, 1953-1961.

Bent, Arthur C., *Life Histories of North American Birds* (23 vols.). Available in paperback. Dover, 1962-1964.

Delacour, J., and P. Scott, *The Waterfowl of the World* (3 vols.). Country Life, 1954-1960.

Fisher, James, and R. M. Lockley, *Seabirds*. Collins, 1954.

Greenewalt, Crawford H., *Hummingbirds*. Doubleday, 1960.

Griscom, L., and A. Sprunt, *The Warblers of North America*. Devin-Adair, 1957.

Kortright, F. H., *Ducks, Geese and Swans of North America*. American Wildlife Institute, 1942.

Murphy, R. C., *Oceanic Birds of South America* (2 vols.). American Museum of Natural History, 1936.

Skutch, A. F., *Life Histories of Central American Birds* (2 vols.). Cooper Ornithological Society, 1954-1960.

Behavior and Communication

Armstrong, E. A., *Bird Display and Behavior*. Lindsay Drummond, 1947.

Cornell Laboratory of Ornithology, *A Field Guide to Bird Songs; A Field Guide to Western Bird Songs* and numerous other recordings. Houghton Mifflin.

Howard, E., *Territory in Bird Life*. Collins, 1948.

Lanyon, W. E., and W. N. Tavolga, eds., *Animal Sounds and Communication*. American Institute of Biological Sciences, 1960.

Lorenz, K. Z., *King Solomon's Ring*. Crowell, 1952.

Saunders, Aretas A., *A Guide to Bird Songs*. Doubleday, 1959.

Thorpe, W. H., *Bird Song*. Cambridge University Press, 1961.

Thorpe, William H., *Learning and Instinct in Animals*. Harvard University Press, 1956.

Tinbergen, Niko, *Bird Life*. Oxford University Press, 1954.

Flight and Migration

Dorst, Jean, *The Migrations of Birds*. Houghton Mifflin, 1963.

Lincoln, Frederick C., *The Migration of Birds*. Doubleday, 1952.

Matthews, G.V.T., *Bird Navigation*. Cambridge University Press, 1955.

Ecology and Population

Craighead, John and Frank, *Hawks, Owls and Wildlife*. Stackpole, 1956.

Elton, Charles S., *The Ecology of Invasions*. John Wiley and Sons, 1958.

Lack, David, *The Natural Regulation of Animal Numbers*. Oxford University Press, 1954.

Odum, Eugene P., *Fundamentals of Ecology*. Saunders, 1959.

Wynne-Edwards, V. C., *Animal Dispersion in Relation to Social Behavior*. Oliver and Boyd, 1962.

Conservation

Gabrielson, Ira N., *Wildlife Conservation*. Macmillan, 1959.

Greenway, James C., Jr., *Extinct and Vanishing Birds of the World*. American Committee for International Wildlife Protection, 1958.

Mathiessen, Peter, *Wildlife in America*. Viking Press, 1959.

Index

Numerals in italics indicate a photograph or painting of the subject mentioned.